GROVER CLEVELAND'S RUBBER JAW AND OTHER UNUSUAL, UNEXPECTED, UNBELIEVABLE BUT ALL-TRUE FACTS ABOUT AMERICA'S PRESIDENTS

BOOKS BY STEPHEN SPIGNESI

Mayberry, My Hometown

The Complete Stephen King Encyclopedia

The Stephen King Quiz Book

The Second Stephen King Quiz Book

The Woody Allen Companion

The Official *Gone With the Wind* Companion

The V. C. Andrews Trivia and Quiz Book

The Odd Index

What's Your *Mad About You* IQ?

The Gore Galore Video Quiz Book

What's Your *Friends* IQ?

The Celebrity Baby Name Book

The *ER* Companion

J.F.K. Jr.

The Robin Williams Scrapbook

The Italian 100

The Beatles Book of Lists

Young Kennedys: The New Generation *(as Jay David Andrews)*

The Lost Work of Stephen King

The Complete *Titanic*

How to Be an Instant Expert

She Came in Through the Kitchen Window:
Recipes Inspired by The Beatles & Their Music

The USA Book of Lists

The UFO Book of Lists

The Essential Stephen King

The Cat Book of Lists

The Hollywood Book of Lists

The Evil 100 *(as Martin Gilman Wolcott)*

Gems, Jewels, & Treasures

Catastrophe! The 100 Greatest Disasters of All Time

In the Crosshairs: 75 Assassinations and Assassination Attempts, from Julius Caesar to John Lennon

Crop Circles: Signs of Contact *(with Colin Andrews)*

Here, There and Everywhere: The 100 Best Beatles Songs *(with Michael Lewis)*

The Weird 100

American Firsts

What's Your Red, White & Blue IQ?

Dialogues: A Novel of Suspense

Second Homes for Dummies *(with Bridget McRae)*

George Washington's Leadership Lessons *(with James Rees)*

From Michelangelo to Mozzarella: The Complete Italian IQ Test

Native American History for Dummies *(with Dorothy Lippert)*

Lost Books of the Bible for Dummies *(with Daniel Smith-Christopher)*

The Third Act of Life *(with Jerome Ellison)*

The *Titanic* for Dummies

GROVER CLEVELAND'S RUBBER JAW

AND OTHER UNUSUAL, UNEXPECTED, UNBELIEVABLE BUT ALL-TRUE FACTS ABOUT AMERICA'S PRESIDENTS

★ STEPHEN SPIGNESI ★

A PERIGEE BOOK

A PERIGEE BOOK
Published by the Penguin Group
Penguin Group (USA) Inc.
375 Hudson Street, New York, New York 10014, USA
Penguin Group (Canada), 90 Eglinton Avenue East, Suite 700, Toronto, Ontario M4P 2Y3, Canada (a division of Pearson Penguin Canada Inc.) • Penguin Books Ltd., 80 Strand, London WC2R 0RL, England • Penguin Group Ireland, 25 St. Stephen's Green, Dublin 2, Ireland (a division of Penguin Books Ltd.) • Penguin Group (Australia), 250 Camberwell Road, Camberwell, Victoria 3124, Australia (a division of Pearson Australia Group Pty. Ltd.) • Penguin Books India Pvt. Ltd., 11 Community Centre, Panchsheel Park, New Delhi—110 017, India • Penguin Group (NZ), 67 Apollo Drive, Rosedale, Auckland 0632, New Zealand (a division of Pearson New Zealand Ltd.) • Penguin Books (South Africa) (Pty.) Ltd., 24 Sturdee Avenue, Rosebank, Johannesburg 2196, South Africa

Penguin Books Ltd., Registered Offices: 80 Strand, London WC2R 0RL, England

First edition: May 2012

Library of Congress Cataloging-in-Publication Data

Spignesi, Stephen J.
Grover Cleveland's rubber jaw, and other unusual, unexpected, unbelievable but all-true facts about America's presidents / Stephen Spignesi. —1st ed.
p. cm.
"A Perigee book."
Includes bibliographical references.
ISBN 978-0-399-53743-1
1. Presidents—United States—Biography—Miscellanea. 2. Presidents—United States—History—Miscellanea. 3. Curiosities and wonders—United States—History—Miscellanea. I. Title.
E176.1.S6973 2012
973.09'9—dc23
[B] 2012000855

PRINTED IN THE UNITED STATES OF AMERICA

10 9 8 7 6 5 4 3 2 1

For Valerie

Anyone who is capable of getting themselves made President should on no account be allowed to do the job.

—DOUGLAS ADAMS

Any man who has had the job I've had and didn't have a sense of humor wouldn't still be here.

—HARRY S TRUMAN

I'm the president and I don't have to eat broccoli if I don't want to.

—GEORGE H. W. BUSH

CONTENTS

INTRODUCTION

The presidents of the United States are, as a group, the most famous Americans of all. There are other Americans who are legendary: Nathan Hale, Davy Crockett, Babe Ruth, Neil Armstrong, J. P. Morgan, Thomas Edison, Douglas MacArthur, Mark Twain, Albert Einstein (he became a U.S. citizen in 1940), but those men are solitary figures. The presidency is different—in fact, unique. The men (no women so far) who fill the position are invested by the public with godlike stature because of the power and dignity of the office. Before and after holding office, the people who serve as president of the United States are mere mortals. But while they occupy the Oval Office in the White House, they are the chief executive, chief of state, and commander in chief of the greatest nation in history, and that brings an awesome stature to them in the eyes of the public, both in America and in the world.

Yet even though these men are the most vetted, public, and famous Americans ever, do we really know all there is to know about them? For example, did you know that President Chester A. Arthur had eighty pairs of pants? Or that Calvin

Coolidge would have Vaseline rubbed onto his head while he ate breakfast in bed?

The American presidents were, of course, ordinary men. Humans like the rest of us. And thus they had what Woody Allen once described as "quirks and mannerisms," as do we all.

Regarding the criteria I used to determine whether a presidential (or First Lady) fact deserved inclusion in this book, I really didn't have a carved-in-stone set of rules. Yes, this makes inclusion relatively subjective, but I did apply certain standards. If it was odd to me, and I felt that nine out of ten people would say something along the lines of "Are you kidding?" if I told it to them, then it made it into the book. However, I did err on the side of inclusion if a presidential fact was especially interesting, intriguing, or relevant to today's world, but not necessarily odd. I believe that including these additional facts satisfies the "I did not know that" criteria I tried to apply to every presidential detail I came across. Plus anything that adds to our knowledge of history can't hurt!

My goal with *Grover Cleveland's Rubber Jaw* was to have fun with history and to teach readers about little-known aspects of the lives of the American presidents. Thus my choices of facts to include are often humorous or surprising.

And the president-themed anagram quiz is included for fun and to keep your brain sharp!

So enjoy this good-hearted look at the most famous people in American history: the presidents of the United States.

GROVER CLEVELAND'S RUBBER JAW AND OTHER UNUSUAL, UNEXPECTED, UNBELIEVABLE BUT ALL-TRUE FACTS ABOUT AMERICA'S PRESIDENTS

THE PRESIDENTS OF THE UNITED STATES

★★★★★★★★★★ ★★★★★★★★★★★

1789–2012

CHAPTER ONE

GEORGE WASHINGTON

1789–1797 (Federalist)

Born: February 22, 1732

Died: December 14, 1799

Cause of Death: Pneumonia. Washington had gone horseback riding in cold, snowy weather, and the following day he complained of a sore throat. This was the beginning of his demise. He was initially diagnosed as suffering from inflammatory quinsy, an inflammation of the tonsils often marked by abscesses. Washington's condition was gravely aggravated by his doctors' "treatments": They bled him with leeches four separate times and raised blisters on his throat and legs as a counterirritant.

Presidential Term: April 30, 1789–March 3, 1797

Age at Inauguration: 57 years, 67 days

Vice President: John Adams

Married: Martha Dandridge Custis on January 6, 1759

Children: John "Jack" Parke Custis (adopted), Martha "Patsy" Custis (adopted)

Religion: Episcopalian

Education: No formal education

Occupation: Planter, soldier, brewer, distiller

GEORGE WASHINGTON was a teenage spelunker. (A spelunker is someone who explores and studies caves.)

By the time he was thirty, Washington had had smallpox, pleurisy, dysentery, and malaria.

It's highly likely that Washington was sterile. Medical experts and historians point to his never having impregnated Martha in their entire forty-year marriage and suspect that the likely culprit for his sterility was his having contracted smallpox when he was young.

Washington was not the first president of the United States. (He was the first president under the U.S. Constitution, though.) In 1781, Maryland ratified the Articles of Federation and Maryland's John Hanson signed the document. Hanson was then elected "President of the United States in Congress Assembled." As evidence of the acceptance of Hanson as president of the United States, a thank-you note exists from then-general

Washington to Hanson in which Washington addresses Hanson as "President of the United States."

When the U.S. capital was moved to Philadelphia, Washington had his slave Hercules sent from Mount Vernon to cook for him. However, Pennsylvania law said that after six months of residence, slaves had to be freed. Rather than lose his excellent cook, Washington would return Hercules to Mount Vernon before the six months were up to outsmart the law. Hercules put up with this for a brief time and ultimately fled to freedom. Washington never saw him again.

Iconic painting notwithstanding, Washington never prayed in the snow at Valley Forge.

In 1775, Washington and his entire household were inoculated against smallpox, thanks to a suggestion by one of Cotton Mather's slaves. In 1775, nearly half of the people in the American colonies were disfigured from smallpox scars, and the disease was still widespread. One of Mather's slaves explained to a minister that natives back home in the African bush also suffered from smallpox, but they had come up with a way of protecting themselves. They would poke a sharp stick into the center of a smallpox pustule on someone with the disease and then stick the point of the stick into the arms of other natives who were not yet infected. The natives were intuitively implementing the proven practice of allowing the body to build up antibodies to resist a disease by using the bacteria or virus itself, the foundation of modern vaccination theory. After hearing of this clever practice, Washington had it done to himself and his entire household.

Washington was one of the eight presidents who owned slaves during his administration. The others were Thomas Jefferson, James Madison, James Monroe, John Tyler, James Polk, Zachary Taylor, and Andrew Jackson.

Washington's nicknames included the American Fabius, the Farmer President, the Father of His Country, the Old Fox, the Sage of Mount Vernon, the Savior of His Country, the Surveyor President, the Sword of the Revolution, the Potomac Stallion, and the Stepfather of His Country.

One of Washington's sets of false teeth was made of eight human teeth taken from dead soldiers and attached to a piece of carved hippopotamus ivory with solid gold rivets. Washington would often remove his dentures to eat. Washington's dentures were never made of wood as often misstated.

Speaking of teeth, when Washington was inaugurated, he had a grand total of one tooth in his mouth.

Washington made sure his horses' teeth were brushed every day.

The Iroquois Indians' nickname for Washington was Caunotaucarius. This means "Devourer of Villages." Obviously, the Iroquois were not big fans of the first president.

After Washington's inauguration, the United States had to decide how to address its new leader. The title originally suggested by a Senate committee was "His Highness the President of the United States of America and Protector of the Rights of Same." (That would make an amazing letterhead, don't you think?) Ultimately, "Mr. President" was deemed more than sufficient. And it has been ever since.

Martha Washington's nickname for her husband was "Pappa," even though he was younger than she was.

Washington introduced the donkey to America.

There are seven mountains in America named after Washington.

In 1798, the year after he left the presidency, Washington was the most prolific distiller in America. His Mount Vernon distillery produced eleven thousand gallons of whiskey that year.

One of Washington's lady friends wrote in her diary of her "womanly admiration" of his "noble exterior."

Washington's second inaugural address is the shortest on record at only 135 words. In its entirety it read:

> Fellow Citizens: I am again called upon by the voice of my country to execute the functions of its Chief Magistrate. When the occasion proper for it shall arrive, I shall endeavor to express the high sense I entertain of this distinguished honor, and of the confidence which has been reposed in me by the people of united America. Previous to the execution of any official act of the President the Constitution requires an oath of office. This oath I am now about to take, and in your presence: That if it shall be found during my administration of the Government I have in any instance violated willingly or knowingly the injunctions thereof, I may (besides incurring constitutional punishment) be subject to the upbraidings of all who are now witnesses of the present solemn ceremony.

Washington is one of the two highest-ranking military officers in the history of the United States. In 1976, President Gerald Ford posthumously awarded Washington with the title general of the armies of the United States. This outranks even five-star generals. (John J. Pershing is the only other general of the armies.)

Washington earned $25,000 a year salary as president of the United States. According to www.measuringworth.com, this compares to more than $615,000 today, based on the Consumer Price Index. (Based on the Unskilled Wage Index, it would be close to a million dollars.) He spent almost two grand of his salary on alcohol, comparable to almost $50,000 today.

Washington was the only president in U.S. history to get a unanimous vote by the electoral college. And he did it twice.

When Martha Washington's loathed ex-father-in-law Daniel Custis died, she went to his mansion and smashed his beloved hand-blown wineglasses.

Washington wouldn't shake hands. He felt it was beneath the dignity of the president.

Washington was an athlete, a great dancer, and a gambler. Legend has it he would bet on anything.

The medical treatment Washington received on his soon-to-be deathbed consisted of being bled numerous times; being made to drink a tonic of vinegar, butter, and molasses; and being pumped full of laxatives. (Do you think one of his final prayers was, "Kill me now, Lord. Please!"?)

Washington's last words were "I am just going. Have me decently buried and do not let my body be put into a vault in less than two days after I am dead. Do you understand me? 'Tis well." Washington was terribly frightened—and had been all his life—of being buried alive. He was essentially telling his people "make sure I'm good and dead before you put me in a grave, please." The extra days would give him a chance to come to, so to speak, in case he had been inaccurately pronounced dead. (He wasn't.)

When Washington died, his wife, Martha, did her best to burn almost all his letters. A few survived, however, and ended up a century later at the J. P. Morgan Library. However, these letters, too, were burned, this time by the Morgan librarian. She said they were "smutty."

Washington has been played in movies by Duke R. Lee, Frank Windsor, Jeff Daniels, and Terry Layman.

CHAPTER TWO

JOHN ADAMS

1797–1801 (Federalist)

Born: October 30, 1735

Died: July 4, 1826

Cause of Death: Heart failure and pneumonia. Adams's death culminated a period of deterioration that confined him to his home and prevented him from attending the celebration marking the fiftieth anniversary of the creation of the United States.

Presidential Term: March 4, 1797–March 3, 1801

Age at Inauguration: 61 years, 125 days

Vice President: Thomas Jefferson

Married: Abigail Smith on October 25, 1764

Children: Abigail Amelia Adams, John Quincy Adams, Susanna Adams, Charles Adams, Thomas Boylston Adams

Religion: Unitarian

Education: Harvard College, graduated 1755

Occupation: Lawyer

JOHN ADAMS once boasted that his family had cut down more trees in America than any other.

Adams started smoking when he was eight years old.

On March 5, 1770, a group of British soldiers opened fire on a group of colonists in Boston. Five men died. This became known as the Boston Massacre. The British soldiers were put on trial. Their lawyer? None other than future president of the United States John Adams.

When Adams was attending Harvard, his typical breakfast was beer and bread.

Adams served as an American diplomat before becoming president and traveled to Europe on behalf of the United States. When he arrived in Paris in 1778, he was immediately mistaken for both his cousin Samuel Adams and also for Thomas Paine, the author of *Common Sense*, which was a big hit in Europe. Since he was neither S. Adams nor T. Paine, he tried diligently to explain who he actually was. Nobody believed him, and he was consistently addressed as men he was not.

Adams didn't like the vice presidency. He considered it the "most insignificant office that ever the Invention of Man contrived or his imagination conceived." Receiving a salary of $5,000—one fifth of the president's—probably didn't help his attitude.

Adams's nicknames included the Atlas of Independence, the Colossus of American Independence, the Duke of Braintree, and His Rotundity.

During a visit to France in 1778, a French woman embarrassed Adams by asking him his thoughts on how Adam and Eve learned about sex because there was no one around to instruct them about the facts of life. He became quite flustered, but after he pulled himself together he went off on some elaborate comparison of human beings to magnets.

Adams had a pronounced lisp, and in those pre–speech therapy days, there wasn't much he could do about it. (When the science of speech pathology began to develop over the next century or so, most of the attention was given to stuttering.) Most historians and biographers believe the lisp was from a pronounced lack of teeth. Reportedly, Adams lost all his teeth and refused to wear dentures, thus the lisp.

Adams said he believed in God, but there's no way he could be described as a Christian. He rejected the belief that Jesus was divine, didn't believe in the idea of the Trinity, and refused to accept the infallibility of scripture.

In an attempt to curb his appetite, Adams always insisted that boiled cornmeal pudding be served first before his meal.

Adams didn't like his white servants "playing cards with Negroes."

Upon moving into the still-unfinished White House, Abigail Adams was less than thrilled with the accommodations. She complained that there were no bells to summon the servants (gasp!), and she hung her wet laundry in what would become the East Room.

In 1798, Adams signed into law the four Alien and Sedition Acts. Historians almost unanimously consider this the single biggest mistake of his presidential career. One of the laws allowed the government to deport any alien resident it felt was dangerous to the United States. Another allowed the government to deport aliens if the United States was at war with their home country. And the Sedition Act essentially made it a crime to speak against the government or the president. The Federalists did not feel the Alien and Sedition Acts violated the Bill of Rights. (Obviously, they were wrong.)

Sometime in 1800, a demented citizen walked into the Adams White House and threatened to kill the president. Adams invited him into the Oval Office, talked to him, and apparently placated him enough to squelch the man's murderous rage. Was the intruder then arrested and charged with attempted assassination? Hardly. He was simply sent on his way.

Adams fled Washington the night before Thomas Jefferson's inauguration to completely avoid Jefferson. The two had a long-standing hostility due to Adams's feelings that Jefferson was a bit duplicitous when he was Adams's vice president. The two ultimately did bury the hatchet, though, and reestablished correspondence.

Thomas Jefferson once said of Adams: "He is vain, irritable, and a bad calculator of the force and probable effect of the motives which govern men."

Adams's cause of death was heart failure and pneumonia. However, at the time, the cause of his death was recorded by one of his descendants as "merely the cessation of the functions of a body worn out by age."

Adams's last words were "Thomas Jefferson still survives." In one of the most astonishing coincidences of American history, John Adams and Thomas Jefferson—the two signers of the Declaration of Independence to become U.S. presidents—both died on the same day, July 4, 1826—the fiftieth anniversary of the Declaration of Independence. Ironically, when Adams uttered his final declaration, he did not know that Jefferson had died around five hours earlier.

Adams has been played in movies by William Daniels and Paul Giamatti.

CHAPTER THREE

THOMAS JEFFERSON

1801–1809 (Democratic-Republican)

Born: April 13, 1743

Died: July 4, 1826

Cause of Death: According to www.Monticello.org, Jefferson's likely cause of death was "exhaustion from intense diarrhea, toxemia from a kidney infection, uremia from kidney damage, and finally orthostatic old-age pneumonia" as well as possibly undiagnosed prostate cancer.

Presidential Term: March 4, 1801–March 3, 1809

Age at Inauguration: 57 years, 325 days

Vice Presidents: Aaron Burr, George Clinton

Married: Martha Wayles Skelton on January 1, 1772

Children: Martha Washington Jefferson, Jane Randolph Jefferson, infant son, Mary Jefferson, Lucy Elizabeth Jefferson

Religion: No formal affiliation

Education: College of William and Mary, graduated 1762

Occupation: Lawyer, planter

THOMAS JEFFERSON often had stress-related headaches. When he was twenty, he developed a two-day killer headache after he embarrassed himself in front of a young woman.

Jefferson invented the swivel chair.

When Jefferson was secretary of state, he once had a headache every day from sunrise to sunset for six solid weeks.

Jefferson loved traveling to Europe. One of the reasons was because of the bookstores. They had a much wider variety of tomes and at much better prices than in American shops. He would spend hours browsing through stores and usually purchasing anything having to do with America.

Jefferson's personal library of ten thousand volumes was of such importance that after the British burned the Library of Congress in 1814, Jefferson offered his own collection of books as a replacement for what was lost in the fire. Congress

accepted and Jefferson's books are still today a part of the archives of the Library of Congress.

Jefferson was terrified of public speaking. In fact, he hated it so much that during his two terms as president, he delivered precisely two public speeches: his inaugural addresses.

Jefferson's nicknames included the Father of the Declaration of Independence, Long Tom, the Pen of the Revolution, the Philosopher of Democracy, and the Sage of Monticello.

Jefferson's inauguration was the first presidential inauguration to be held in Washington, D.C.

Jefferson did, in fact, walk to his own inauguration wearing a plain gray suit. In later years, Presidents Carter and Clinton would emulate Jefferson by walking to their own inaugurations. Jefferson's stroll has always been perceived as Jefferson's way of proclaiming and proving that he was an ordinary man of the people. The truth is that Jefferson walked because his new $6,000 carriage and handmade velvet suit had not arrived in time for the ceremony.

Jefferson believed that cold foot baths gave him longevity. He may have been on to something: He lived to be eighty-three.

Jefferson introduced French fries to America. He served them in 1802 at a dinner at the White House. He described them to his guests as "potatoes served in the French manner."

Jefferson was an abolitionist who owned lots of slaves. Being the good guy that he was, Jefferson one day freed his cook, James Hemings. This, perhaps surprisingly, did not work out very well for Mr. Hemings, who quickly begged to be taken back. But Jefferson insisted he embrace freedom. Hemings ultimately became an alcoholic and eventually killed himself. (Seeming to disprove Aeschylus when he wrote, "Willingly no one chooses the yoke of slavery.")

Sally Hemings, a slave with whom Jefferson fathered children, was Jefferson's wife's half sister. (Jefferson's father-in-law had impregnated Sally's mother.) Sally was a relative of James Hemings, the cook Jefferson freed.

Jefferson's original rough draft of the Declaration of Independence included the following slam against Great Britain for its role in the slave trade. It was deleted from the final version:

> He has waged cruel war against human nature itself, violating its most sacred rights of life & liberty in the persons of a distant people who never offended him, captivating & carrying them into slavery in another hemisphere, or to incur miserable death in their transportation thither. This piratical warfare, the opprobrium of infidel powers, is the warfare of the Christian king of Great Britain. Determined to keep open a market where MEN should be bought & sold, he has prostituted his negative for suppressing every legislative attempt to prohibit or to restrain this execrable commerce.

Jefferson invented the dumbwaiter.

When Jefferson was forty-three, he crippled his right hand jumping over a fence while out strolling with the married twenty-seven-year-old Maria Cosway, with whom he was having an affair.

As president, Jefferson loved romping with his grandchildren on the White House lawn. When someone mentioned to him how much fun children can provide to adults, Jefferson responded with what might be one of the most perfect analyses of the adult–child dynamic ever when he said, "Yes, it is only with them that a grave man can play the fool."

Jefferson rewrote the New Testament. In his version, known as *The Jefferson Bible* and *The Life and Morals of Jesus of Nazareth* and not published until seventy-five years after his death, he removed all of what would be considered the "paranormal/supernatural" stuff. In his revision, Jesus was a man. He was a brilliant philosopher, ethicist, and humanist and did not call himself the son of God, perform miracles, or rise from the dead. Jefferson admired Jesus' teachings, but believed that all the other sensationalism was added by the Gospel writers. Jefferson's Bible ends with the following passage:

> And there came also Nicodemus, which at the first came to Jesus by night, and brought a mixture of myrrh and aloes, about an hundred pound weight. Then took they the body of Jesus, and wound it in linen clothes with the spices, as the manner of the Jews is to bury. Now in the place where he was crucified there was a garden; and in the garden a new sepulchre, wherein was never man yet laid. There laid they Jesus, and rolled a great stone to the door of the sepulchre, and departed.

Jefferson had to sell his books for $25,000 to alleviate some of his post-presidential debt, but he still died broke—and owing what would be a million bucks in today's dollars. Truth be told, though, part of Jefferson's problems were due to his fondness for elaborate entertaining when he was president. His grocery bill amounted to $50 a day, which today would be $884. He annually spent $1,400 (in 1801 dollars) on champagne and wine alone. That's twenty-five grand in today's dollars. When we consider that he was picking up the tab for all these costs out of his $25,000 annual salary, it's no surprise he died destitute. His heirs had to sell his plantation Monticello to pay off what he owed.

Did you know that Jefferson was also a poet? Two days before he died, he wrote a poem to his daughter, Martha Jefferson Randolph. It is called "A Death-bed Adieu." This touching farewell was originally published in *The Domestic Life of Thomas Jefferson*. As he lay dying, he called her to him and told her where to find the poem he had secreted away.

A DEATH-BED ADIEU FROM TH. J TO M. R.

Life's visions are vanished, its dreams are no more;
Dear friends of my bosom, why bathed in tears?
I go to my fathers, I welcome the shore
Which crowns all my hopes or which buries my cares.
Then farewell, my dear, my lov'd daughter, adieu!
The last pang of life is in parting from you!
Two seraphs await me, long shrouded in death;
I will bear them your love on my last parting breath.

Was Jefferson a vegetarian? Not really, since he did eat meat. However, his primary diet consisted of vegetables. He wrote that he ate meat only "as a condiment to the vegetables which constitute my principal diet." His favorite vegetable was the English (garden) pea.

Jefferson was passionately pro-education. His granddaughter Ellen Wayles Randolph wrote about how he would inculcate a love of learning in his grandchildren.

> He took pains to correct our errors and false ideas, checked the bold, encouraged the timid, and tried to teach us to reason soundly and feel rightly. . . . He was watchful over our manners, and called our attention to every violation of propriety. He did not interfere with our education . . . except by advising us what studies to pursue, what books to read, and by questioning us on the books which we did read.

Jefferson's final days were spent bedridden and suffering with tremendous pain, for which he took the opium-based drug laudanum. The opiate seemed to work. In an account of his grandfather's death, Colonel T. J. Randolph wrote, "He suffered no pain, but gradually sank from debility." Like Adams, Jefferson was too sick to attend the nation's fiftieth birthday party in Washington.

Jefferson's last words were "Is it the Fourth?"

Jefferson refused to allow his two terms as U.S. president to be acknowledged on his tombstone. Instead his tombstone reads:

Here was buried Thomas Jefferson
Author of the Declaration of Independence

Of the Statute of Virginia for Religious Freedom
And Father of the University of Virginia

Some scholars have speculated that of all his achievements, he considered being president beneath authoring the Declaration of Independence, the Virginia Statute for Religious Freedom, and founding the University of Virginia, and thus chose to not even mention it. Today, no matter what a man has done throughout his life, it is universally acknowledged that being president of the United States was his ultimate achievement in life. Also, the magnificent grave marker at Jefferson's Monticello is a copy. The original, which fell into disrepair, was donated by Jefferson's family to the University of Missouri, where it now resides.

Jefferson has been played in movies by Ken Howard and Nick Nolte.

CHAPTER FOUR

JAMES MADISON

1809–1817 (Democratic-Republican)

Born: March 16, 1751

Died: June 28, 1836

Cause of Death: Heart failure, with complications from rheumatism and liver problems and/or gallbladder attacks. Madison was so sick in 1836 that he spent his final six months of life suffering in bed. He was not able to survive until the Fourth of July.

Presidential Term: March 4, 1809–March 3, 1817

Age at Inauguration: 57 years, 353 days

Vice Presidents: George Clinton Madison, Elbridge Gerry Madison

Married: Dolley Payne Todd on September 15, 1794

Children: John Payne Todd (stepson)

Religion: Episcopalian

Education: College of New Jersey (now Princeton University), graduated 1771

Occupation: Lawyer

What do Shania Twain, Barbara Walters, Mae West, Betty White, Madonna, Gustav Mahler, Scarlett Johansson, Alanis Morissette, Pablo Picasso, Britney Spears, Elizabeth Taylor, Drew Barrymore, Mel Brooks, Queen Elizabeth, Michael J. Fox, and Larry Fine and Moe Howard of the Three Stooges have in common with **JAMES MADISON**? They're all five feet, four inches tall. Madison was the shortest president in American history.

For most of his life, Madison never weighed more than 100 pounds. He began gaining a little weight as he aged and was reportedly 121 pounds at the time of his death.

Before the War of 1812, Madison came up with a brilliant idea for avoiding the expense of building more battleships. He wanted to rent Portugal's navy to fight for the United States. It didn't happen.

Madison personally led a military brigade during the War of 1812. He had to order a retreat.

Madison was the first president to wear pants. Boy, that sounds salacious, doesn't it? But it's perfectly innocent, and completely true. Before Madison, men wore knee breeches. Long pants were a new sartorial innovation when Madison became president and he embraced them immediately.

Madison's nicknames included Little Jemmy and His Little Majesty.

Madison's stepson John Payne Todd (Dolley's son from her earlier marriage to John Todd Jr.) was an irresponsible profligate. Madison paid out over $40,000 to Todd's creditors and yet the kid still ended up in debtor's prison twice. (This was in the day when they still had debtor's prisons. "You can't pay your bills? Off to jail you go!") His greed caused problems with the publication of Madison's papers, and when his mother sold some of Madison's possessions to Congress, he threatened to sue if he didn't get access to the money. Congress called his bluff and the money was protected for Dolley. It is said his mother was the only one who liked him and the only one who would put up with him. (That is not hard to believe.)

The U.S. Treasury used to make a $5,000 bill, and Madison was on it.

Dolley Madison once threw a party at which stationary, torch-holding slaves provided the illumination.

What was Madison talking about when he said, "Every word decides a question between power and liberty"? The U.S. Constitution. (Does kind of sum it up, doesn't it?)

Dolley Madison was the first American to respond to a telegram. It was sent to her by none other than Samuel Morse, the inventor of the telegraph.

Madison was George Washington's half first cousin, twice removed.

Dolley Madison was a snuffer. She loved using snuff tobacco and was one of the few women of her time to indulge in the vice openly.

Madison's last words were either "Nothing more than a change of *mind*, my dear," or "I always talk better lying down." Reports are contradictory.

Madison has been played in movies by Burgess Meredith.

CHAPTER FIVE

JAMES MONROE

1817–1825 (Democratic-Republican)

Born: April 28, 1758

Died: July 4, 1831

Cause of Death: Heart failure with possible tuberculosis. In one of those incredible historical coincidences, Monroe was the third of the first five U.S. presidents to die on the Fourth of July.

Presidential Term: March 4, 1817–March 3, 1825

Age at Inauguration: 58 years, 310 days

Vice President: Daniel D. Tompkins

Married: Elizabeth "Eliza" Kortright on February 16, 1786

Children: Eliza Kortright Monroe, James Spence Monroe, Maria Hester Monroe

Religion: Episcopalian

Education: College of William and Mary, graduated 1776

Occupation: Lawyer

JAMES MONROE's law professor was Thomas Jefferson. (Talk about an influential teacher, eh?)

Monroe was the only U.S. president who had been wounded in the Revolutionary War. He was shot in the shoulder and the bullet was never removed.

Monroe was one of the leading supporters of a "send the blacks back to Africa" movement called the American Colonization Society (ACS). After he became president, he saw to it that the goal of the ACS became a reality. The United States bought land in Africa and named it Liberia. The capital was named after Monroe: Monrovia. Ultimately, around 15,000 blacks left the United States and went to Liberia. Of 1.8 million blacks (out of a total U.S. population of 9.6 million), it didn't look like the "send 'em home" movement was going to work. And it didn't. Monrovia still exists, however, as the only African city named after a white American president.

Monroe and Zachary Taylor were second cousins.

Monroe was the first president to ride on a steamboat.

Monroe's nicknames included the Era-of-Good-Feelings President and the Lost Cocked Hat.

Monroe pardoned a number of pirates during his administration.

Monroe's wife, Elizabeth, fell down. A lot. She once fell into a fireplace. A lit fireplace. What was wrong with her? No one knows with absolute certainty because very little was written about her, either when she was alive or after her death, and her letters were all burned. However, the generally accepted wisdom is that she was an epileptic, and because epilepsy was considered a mental illness back then, she did everything in her power to keep her condition a secret.

Monroe voted against ratifying the U.S. Constitution. This sounds radical and anti-American, but truth be told, his reasons were good: He felt the Bill of Rights should have been part of the original Constitution, he felt the Constitution made the Senate too powerful, and he felt the electoral college was a mistake and that the president should have been elected by popular vote.

When Monroe left the White House after his presidency, his political debts were so high he was forced to sell off his slaves and all his property to fend off bankruptcy.

Monroe has been played in movies by Morgan Wallace and Charles Waldron.

CHAPTER SIX

JOHN QUINCY ADAMS

1825–1829 (Democratic-Republican)

Born: July 11, 1767

Died: February 23, 1848

Cause of Death: Stroke. Adams had survived one stroke in 1846, but a second stroke, suffered in February 1848 while Adams was working during a session of Congress, put him into a coma and ultimately killed him two days later.

Presidential Term: March 4, 1825–March 3, 1829

Age at Inauguration: 57 years, 236 days

Vice President: John C. Calhoun

Married: Louisa Catherine Johnson on July 26, 1797

Children: George Washington Adams, John Adams, Charles Francis Adams, Louisa Catherine Adams

Religion: Unitarian

Education: Harvard College, graduated 1787

Occupation: Lawyer

At the age of eight, **JOHN QUINCY ADAMS** reportedly watched the Battle of Bunker Hill from his front porch.

Adams was an interpreter for the United States envoy to Russia at the age of only fourteen.

Every night of his life—including his years as president—before going to sleep, Adams would recite the well-known children's prayer "Now I lay me down to sleep . . ." This prayer first appeared in a grammar school textbook called the *New England Primer* in 1690 in Boston. Adams's favorite bedtime prayer was also a favorite prayer of colonial-era children.

Adams's nicknames included Old Man Eloquent, the Accidental President, and the Abolitionist.

Adams liked to swim naked in the Potomac.

One of Adams's most famous accomplishments doesn't even

have his name on it. Adams is the actual author of the Monroe Doctrine, which declared that European countries could not colonize or interfere with America as it would be viewed as an act of aggression.

Adams loaded a gun twice while teaching his sons about firearms. The gun subsequently blew up when he fired it and damaged his eye. The eye healed. His pride probably did not.

It seems that Adams favored a slovenly personal appearance—that is, he dressed like a slob. It is believed he wore the same hat for ten years.

Adams apparently believed in the Hollow Earth theory. He approved an expedition to the entry hole to the earth's interior at the North Pole, but Andrew Jackson canceled it.

Adams was a published poet. In 1832, his book of poetry *Dermot MacMorrogh or, The Conquest of Ireland: An Historical Tale of the Twelfth Century* was released.

Adams would never have been awarded Father of the Year. He was very hard on his kids and he wouldn't let them come home from school if their grades did not meet with his approval. Of his three sons, one committed suicide and one died of alcoholism.

Adams had a pet alligator. He kept it in the White House bathtub.

What James Buchanan said about Adams: "His disposition is as perverse and mulish as that of his father."

Adams's father was President John Adams. The Adamses and the Bushes are the only two father–son presidents in American history.

Adams once wrote to his wife, "I never was and never shall be . . . a popular man."

If it weren't for Adams, the Smithsonian Institution would not exist. When James Smithson, the son of a British nobleman, died in 1835 and left $10 million (in today's dollars) to the United States, Senator John Calhoun wanted to refuse it. He was still pissed off at the British for setting fire to the White House in 1814. But former president John Quincy Adams would have none of that. He fought to convince Congress to accept the money, and they ultimately did. It then took ten years, though, for them to figure out what to with it. They finally decided on a museum of sorts and eventually built the Smithsonian Institution.

Adams's wife, Louisa, once found one of her son's porn collections. She described it as "disgusting pictures of nature."

Adams's last words were "This is the end of earth," followed by either "but I am composed" or "I am content."

Adams has been played in movies by Grant Mitchell and Anthony Hopkins.

CHAPTER SEVEN

ANDREW JACKSON

1829–1837 (Democrat)

Born: March 15, 1767

Died: June 8, 1845

Cause of Death: Heart failure caused by tuberculosis, dropsy (a pathological accumulation of diluted lymph in body tissues and cavities), and chronic diarrhea. Jackson died six days after doctors performed an operation to drain fluid from his abdomen.

Presidential Term: March 4, 1829–March 3, 1837

Age at Inauguration: 61 years, 354 days

Vice Presidents: John C. Calhoun, Martin Van Buren

Married: Rachel Donelson Robards in August 1791, with a second ceremony on January 17, 1794

Children: Andrew Jackson Jr. (adopted), Lincoya Jackson (adopted)

Religion: Presbyterian

Education: No formal education

Occupation: Lawyer, soldier

As a young man, **ANDREW JACKSON** was known to slobber.

Jackson was the first U.S. president born in a log cabin.

In 1781, while serving in a militia, Jackson, then fourteen, was captured by a British regiment. One of the British soldiers ordered Jackson to clean his boots. Jackson refused, and the British soldier swung a sword at his head to decapitate him for his insolence. Jackson dodged the sword, but was still wounded by the blow. He carried the scar the rest of his life.

Jackson's wife, Rachel, was a bigamist, which made Jackson an adulterer. When he married Rachel Robards in 1791, her divorce from her first husband had not been finalized, and thus she was still married. When this was discovered, Jackson had to remarry her after she was divorced.

To protect his twenty-six slaves from illegal seizure by authorities while on a journey away from his plantation, Jackson removed their chains, armed them with axes and clubs, and marched them past a checkpoint that had been set up as an excuse to confiscate slaves on the premise that they were runaways. After passing the checkpoint, Jackson took back the weapons and put his slaves back into chains.

Jackson had a bullet painfully lodged next to his heart from 1806 until his death in 1845. He had been shot in the chest during a duel with Charles Dickinson, who had insulted Jackson's wife. Jackson sometimes coughed up blood and, to alleviate the pain from the bullet, he would on occasion slit open his own veins with a pocketknife and "bleed" himself.

The mascot of the Democratic Party is the jackass, which came from what Jackson's opponents called him.

Jackson's nicknames included the Hero of New Orleans, King Andrew the First, Mischie-Andy, Old Hickory, the Pointed Arrow, the Sage of the Hermitage, and the Sharp Knife.

Jackson adored his wife, Rachel. She died the year before he became president. He carried a portrait of her in a locket with him for the rest of his life. Every night, he would place the miniature on his bed stand so her face would be the first thing he saw upon awakening in the morning.

After winning the presidential election, Jackson invited anyone from Tennessee who wanted to come to Washington for his inauguration. It is believed that thirty thousand or more people accepted his invitation and an enormous mob descended on the town, and every last one of them wanted to get into the White House and shake the new president's hand. Ultimately, the back-home crowd trashed the White House mercilessly and the partying got so intense, the new president spent the night at a hotel while his staff tried to get his guests out of the White House. Congress eventually had to allocate $50,000 for repairs and new furniture. Carpets, too. Apparently it's pretty difficult to get tobacco juice, whiskey, and squished chicken out of a rug.

Jackson did not like being addressed as "Mr. President." He preferred "General."

As a slave owner, Jackson didn't fool around. His slaves were his property and he wouldn't tolerate losing even one of them. When one of his slaves ran away, he posted the following ad in the newspaper:

> 1804: Stop the Runaway. FIFTY DOLLARS REWARD. Eloped from the subscriber, living near Nashville, on the 25th of June last, a Mulatto Man Slave . . . ten dollars extra, for every hundred lashes, any person will give him, to the amount of three hundred.

In an episode of the TV series *The West Wing*, Chief of Staff Leo McGarry designated one day a year as "Big Block of Cheese Day," in honor of Jackson. Leo claimed that Jackson had a two-ton block of cheese in the foyer of his White House and that it was free to anyone who was hungry. The gist of the story is true, though it was not a regular practice. In 1837, Jackson was gifted with a block of cheese weighing fourteen hundred pounds. He let the cheese age for two years and then, in 1839, he invited citizens to come to the White House and taste his cheese. Fourteen hundred pounds of cheese were eaten in two hours. That's twelve pounds of cheese per minute. At two ounces per person, that means almost twelve thousand people attended Jackson's White House cheese-o-rama.

The U.S. government under Jackson was completely debt free for the first and only time in American history.

Jackson fought in both the American Revolution and the War of 1812.

Jackson got into many duels throughout his life and usually volunteered to let the other guy fire first.

Jackson was not a fan of proper spelling. One of his more memorable comments on the situation was, "It's a damn small mind that can think of only one way to spell a word." (See Theodore Roosevelt, father of the Simplified Spelling Board, for more presidential musings on spelling [page 126].)

Jackson may have believed that the world was flat. He was the one who canceled the John Quincy Adams–approved journey to the center of the earth. (John Quincy was apparently a Hollow Earther.)

What John Quincy Adams said about Jackson: "[He is] a barbarian who cannot write a sentence of grammar and can hardly spell his own name."

On Friday, January 30, 1835, a mentally ill painter named Richard Lawrence fired two guns at Jackson up close and personal. Both guns misfired, so Jackson then proceeded to beat Lawrence with his cane. Lawrence was arrested and tried. The prosecutor was none other than Francis Scott Key, composer of "The Star-Spangled Banner." Lawrence ended up in a mental institution where he died twenty-six years after his assassination attempt on Jackson.

Jackson's favorite food was turkey hash.

As president, Jackson ordered twenty spittoons for the White House at a cost of $12.50 each. The idea behind them was to help preserve the White House carpets. (Gross.)

Smoking gave Jackson headaches. But he kept smoking.

Jackson's last words were "Oh, do not cry. Be good children, and we shall all meet in Heaven."

Jackson has been played in movies by Charlton Heston (twice), Basil Ruysdael, Dave McArdle, and G. D. Spradlin.

CHAPTER EIGHT

MARTIN VAN BUREN

1837–1841 (Democrat)

Born: December 5, 1782

Died: July 24, 1862

Cause of Death: Heart failure caused by complications from chronic bronchial asthma.

Presidential Term: March 4, 1837–March 3, 1841

Age at Inauguration: 54 years, 89 days

Vice President: Richard M. Johnson

Married: Hannah Hoes on February 21, 1807

Children: Abraham Van Buren, John Van Buren, Martin Van Buren, Wilfield Scott, Smith Thompson Van Buren, unnamed stillborn daughter

Religion: Dutch Reformed

Education: Kinderhook Academy, graduated 1796

Occupation: Lawyer

MARTIN VAN BUREN was the first president who was born a U.S. citizen.

When Van Buren was vice president to Andrew Jackson and president pro tempore of the Senate, he presided over sessions of the Senate with two pistols strapped to his legs. It seems that Senate sessions had a tendency to get a tad violent back then and Van Buren wanted to be ready in case gunplay was necessary.

Van Buren drank soot and charcoal in water as a stomach aid.

Twelve sitting U.S. presidents have met with the pope over the years. Van Buren met with Pope Pius IX in 1855, but he had been out of office for fourteen years.

Van Buren was only five feet, six inches tall and was described as a "little squirt."

Depending on how you feel about its ubiquitous usage these days, you can either thank or deride Van Buren for his responsibility in bringing the term *okay* into being. Van Buren was from Kinderhook, New York, and was nicknamed Old Kinderhook. This became "OK," which Van Buren's people chose to associate with him being an "all right kind of guy." The connection stuck.

When Van Buren wrote his autobiography, he mentioned his wife, Hannah, a total of zero times.

Van Buren's nicknames included the Albany Regency, the American Tallyrand, the Enchanter, the Fox, Kinderhook Fox, King Martin the First, the Little Magician, Little Van, Machievellian Belshazzar, Matty Van, the Mistletoe Politician, Petticoat Pet, the Red Fox of Kinderhook, Martin Van Ruin, the Sage of Lindenwald, and Whiskey Van.

Van Buren's first language was not English. It was Dutch. When he got worked up, a slight Dutch accent crept into his pronunciation.

In 1838, Governor Lilburn Boggs of Missouri issued an order that force could be used to remove twenty thousand Mormons from the state. Mormons were not welcome in Missouri. None other than Joseph Smith Jr., the founder of Mormonism, met with Van Buren in 1839 to request his help at getting the order rescinded. According to Van Buren's nephew, the president told Smith, "Your cause is just, but I can do nothing for you; if I take up for you I shall lose the vote of Missouri."

Van Buren was something of a neat freak. He was a clothes horse and always wore the latest fashions. In fact, Van Buren was so meticulous about his appearance that he would often deny himself necessities so he could buy the newest clothes. There were also rumors he wore a corset to maintain a slim appearance.

Memorable or not as a president, one of Van Buren's quotes can undeniably be considered wisdom for the ages and is as true today as . . . well, as it always was: "It is easier to do a job right than to explain why you didn't."

Van Buren earned an annual salary of $25,000 as president. For the entire four years of his term, he accepted not a cent of his pay. At the end of his term, he received the entire $100,000 in one lump sum.

During dinner at the White House one evening, a waiter bent over and whispered to Van Buren that the kitchen was on fire. Van Buren calmly excused himself, and went to put the fire out by organizing a bucket brigade. Reportedly, that was the only time he had ever set foot in the White House kitchen.

Van Buren moved to Sorrento, Italy, when he was in his seventies to write his memoirs. He had learned about Italy from reading James Fenimore Cooper's *Gleanings in Europe: Italy.*

Van Buren's funeral procession consisted of eighty carriages, yet no bells tolled for the departed president. Van Buren had left specific instructions that he did not want any bells to toll at his funeral.

Van Buren once said, "As to the Presidency, the two happiest days of my life were those of my entrance upon the office and my surrender of it."

Van Buren has been played in a movie by Nigel Hawthorne.

CHAPTER NINE

WILLIAM HENRY HARRISON

1841 (Whig)

Born: February 9, 1773

Died: April 4, 1841

Cause of Death: Heart failure caused by complications from pneumonia, initially diagnosed by his doctors as "bilious pleurisy."

Presidential Term: March 4, 1841–April 4, 1841

Age at Inauguration: 68 years, 23 days

Vice President: John Tyler

Married: Anna Tuthill Symmes on November 25, 1795

Children: Elizabeth Bassett Harrison, John Cleves Symmes Harrison, Lucy Singleton Harrison, William Henry Harrison, John Scott Harrison, Benjamin Harrison, Mary Symmes Harrison, Carter Bassett Harrison, Anna Tuthill Harrison, James Findlay Harrison, Dilsia (daughter of one of his slaves)

Religion: Episcopalian

Education: Hampden-Sydney College, attended

Occupation: Soldier

WILLIAM HENRY HARRISON was the last American president who was born a British subject.

Harrison's family was attacked by a regiment led by Benedict Arnold during the Revolutionary War. Everyone survived, but Arnold's soldiers plundered the Harrison farm.

In 1791, Harrison dropped out of medical school to join the army. He wanted to be a doctor but couldn't afford the education.

Harrison's son John Scott Harrison died in 1878, and his body was stolen within twenty-four hours of being buried. One of John Scott's sons and a friend traveled to Ohio Medical College, suspecting that John Scott's body had been stolen for medical research. They were right and found the body hanging by a rope beneath a trapdoor at the medical school. Another of John Scott's sons, Benjamin Harrison, became the twenty-third president of the United States.

What Martin Van Buren said about Harrison: "He does not seem to realize the vast importance of his elevation. . . . He is as tickled with the Presidency as a young man with a new bonnet."

Harrison's nicknames included the Farmer President, the Log Cabin Candidate, Old Granny, Tippecanoe, and the Washington of the West.

Harrison was less than confident about his chances of being elected president. He said, "I am the clerk of the Court of Common Pleas of Hamilton County at your service. . . . Some folks are silly enough to have formed a plan to make a president of the U.S. out of this clerk and clodhopper."

Harrison had eleven children and a goat.

Harrison had 48 grandchildren and 106 great-grandchildren. He wins the prize as the president with the most of each.

Harrison issued no presidential pardons during his administration.

Harrison's inaugural address is the longest on record at around eight-four hundred words. It took him one hour, forty-five minutes to deliver it. In a snowstorm. Harrison insisted on giving his inaugural address outside without a coat or hat. After this he got caught in a downpour and caught a cold, which progressively worsened and ultimately killed him. Harrison's administration—all of thirty-two days—was the shortest in U.S. history. He died of pneumonia a month later.

Harrison was the first U.S. president to die in office.

Harrison's last words were "I wish you to understand the true principles of the Government. I wish them carried out. I ask nothing more."

Harrison has been played in movies by James Seay, Wolfgang Greese, and David Clennon.

CHAPTER TEN

JOHN TYLER

1841–1845 (Whig)

Born: March 29, 1790

Died: January 18, 1862

Cause of Death: Heart failure from gallbladder and/or liver problems and bronchitis.

Presidential Term: April 6, 1841–March 3, 1845

Age at Inauguration: 51 years, 6 days

Vice President: None. (At the time, there was no Constitutional mechanism to replace a vice president who ascended to the presidency, thus the position remained vacant.)

Married: Letitia Christian on March 29, 1813; Julia Gardiner on June 26, 1844

Children: Mary Tyler, Robert Tyler, John Tyler, Letitia Tyler, Elizabeth Tyler, Anne Contesse Tyler, Alice Tyler, Tazewell Tyler, David Gardiner Tyler, John Alexander Tyler, Julia Gardiner Tyler, Lachlan Tyler, Lyon Gardiner Tyler, Robert Fitzwalter Tyler, Pearl Tyler

Religion: Episcopalian

Education: College of William and Mary, graduated 1807

Occupation: Lawyer

JOHN TYLER ascended to the presidency after the death in office of William Henry Harrison. Because this occurred in the days before the Twenty-Fifth Amendment and the 1886 Presidential Succession Act, there were those who did not consider Tyler a real president. This did not sit well with Tyler, and he made his feelings known. Whenever something was sent to the White House addressed to the "Acting President," he refused it and sent it back with "Addressee Unknown" written on the envelope.

Tyler was fifty-four when he married twenty-three-year-old Julia Gardiner. He described her as "raven-haired, with a radiant complexion, an hourglass waist, and a full bust." Shortly after his marriage to Julia, Tyler withdrew from running for a second term and retired to his Virginia estate with his new young wife. Seven of Tyler's fifteen children were with Julia, who gave birth once every two years for fourteen years straight.

When William Henry Harrison died, the Constitution was vague on whether the vice president actually became the president, or was only acting president until an election could be held. Tyler unilaterally decided that the former was the case and immediately established that upon a president's death or removal from office, the vice president was the new president.

Tyler was the most fertile president of all time. He fathered fifteen children with two wives.

One of Tyler's illustrious White House visitors was Charles Dickens, who remarked that the building looked "like an English clubhouse."

During his presidency, Tyler refused to name a vice president. He served his entire term without one.

During Tyler's term, a raging epidemic of influenza terrorized the country. The outbreak was known as the "Tyler grippe." (Presidents get blamed for everything, don't they?)

On Wednesday, February 28, 1844, a huge gun exploded on the deck of the warship USS *Princeton*. The twelve-inch cannon was called the Peacemaker and it fired a 225-pound cannonball. The gun's effective distance was five miles and it used 50 pounds of gunpowder for each firing. Tyler was onboard when the gun exploded. He had previously witnessed two successful firings of the gun and was, presumably, dutifully impressed. The president was belowdecks when it was announced that there would be one more firing, the third that day, and he began to climb up to witness the spectacle yet again. But then his son-in-law began singing a military song and, to be polite, Tyler paused on the ladder so he wouldn't leave the room during the singing. Meanwhile the gun was fired; only this time it exploded. Eight people were killed and twenty more seriously injured. The Washington paper *Daily National Intelligencer* headlined their story about the tragedy with "Most Awful and Most Lamentable Catastrophe!" A military song saved the life of President Tyler.

Tyler officially supported slavery, but once became physically ill upon witnessing a slave auction.

Tyler was an accomplished violinist.

Tyler's nicknames included the Accidental President and His Accidency.

What James Buchanan said about Tyler: "A Manifesto . . . will appear tomorrow from the Whigs in Congress reading John Tyler out of the Whig Church and delivering him over to Satan to be buffeted."

Tyler was elected to the Confederate House of Representatives sixteen years after his presidential administration ended. He died before taking his seat in the House.

Tyler had the following inscribed on the headstone of his horse, The General: "Here lies the body of my good horse 'The General.' For twenty years he bore me around the circuit of my practice, and in all that time he never made a blunder. Would that his master could say the same! John Tyler."

Tyler was uncomfortable around what one biographer described as "people with dirty fingernails." This gave him a reputation of being a snob but it was probably more that he was insecure and had never been around what the *Titanic* crew would have probably described as "Third Class people."

After serving as president, Tyler was elected to the Virginia House of Representatives, as a Confederate. He is the only U.S. president to serve in the Confederacy.

Tyler's last words were "Doctor, I am going. Perhaps it is best."

At his request, Tyler was buried with his coffin draped with the Confederate flag.

Tyler has never been portrayed in a movie.

CHAPTER ELEVEN

JAMES POLK

1845–1849 (Democrat)

Born: November 2, 1795

Died: June 15, 1849

Cause of Death: Cholera (an acute, infectious, often epidemic disease characterized by watery diarrhea, vomiting, cramps, and suppression of urine). Polk died a mere three months after retiring from the presidency.

Presidential Term: March 4, 1845–March 3, 1849

Age at Inauguration: 49 years, 122 days

Vice President: George M. Dallas

Married: Sarah Childress on January 1, 1824

Children: None

Religion: Presbyterian

Education: University of North Carolina, graduated 1818

Occupation: Lawyer

JAMES POLK had excruciatingly painful kidney stones when he was sixteen years old. His surgeon gave him a shot of brandy and operated. The surgery was successful, but left him sterile. (And probably remembering for the rest of his life what it felt like to be operated on without anesthesia.)

Polk was the Anti-Delegator. He refused to delegate any of his work to anyone else. He apparently had trust issues.

Polk may have been the only American president to fulfill every one of his campaign promises. While running for president, Polk promised to acquire California from Mexico, settle the Oregon dispute, lower taxes, establish a subtreasury, and serve only four years. When he left office in 1849, he had accomplished everything he had promised.

Polk liked to carry his money around with him in a suitcase. His wife tried to persuade him to put it in a bank, but she couldn't convince him.

Polk loathed shaking hands.

According to people who saw him frequently, Polk seemed to always be tired.

Polk's nicknames included the First Dark Horse, the Napoleon of the Stump, and Young Hickory.

Due to his contraction of cholera, it is believed that Polk suffered from chronic diarrhea every day of his administration. Ultimately the cholera killed him shortly after the end of his presidential term.

He had nothing to do with it, but in 1846, during Polk's administration, the crack in the Liberty Bell widened enough that the bell never rang again.

Polk was probably a rather dull conversationalist. He wouldn't talk about anything but politics and considered vacations anathema.

What Andrew Jackson said about Polk: "Polk's appointments all in all are the most damnable set that was ever made by any President since the government was organized."

Polk was the first president for whom "Hail to the Chief" was played ceremonially. The song had been previously played at the White House during the Jackson, Van Buren, and Tyler administrations, but Polk's inauguration was the first time it was played to herald a specific president.

Polk had gaslights installed in the White House so he could work until the wee hours.

Sarah Polk was very frugal with her husband's presidential salary of $25,000. She got around spending money by using slaves to do the required work around the White House. At one point she said, "The writers of the Declaration of Independence were mistaken when they affirmed that all men are created equal." She claimed that slaves "toiling in the heat of the sun" were "created for [that place]."

Sarah Polk was a prude and possibly a religious fanatic. She considered dancing utterly ungodly and wouldn't even set foot in a room where such hedonistic behavior was going on.

President Polk's term concluded at the end of the day on Saturday, March 3, 1849. His vice president, George Dallas, had already resigned his office by then, and the normal sequence of events would have been for the incoming president to be sworn in immediately. Zachary Taylor refused to be sworn in on a Sunday, however, so the official chain of succession decreed that the president pro tempore of the Senate, David Atchison, was acting president of the United States. Atchison later told a reporter that he spent his only day in office napping. His tombstone reads, "President of the United States for One Day."

Polk was baptized one week before his death.

Polk has been played in movies by Edwin Stanley, Ian Wolfe, and Addison Richards.

CHAPTER TWELVE

ZACHARY TAYLOR

1849–1850 (Whig)

Born: November 24, 1784

Died: July 9, 1850

Cause of Death: Systemic failure with gastrointestinal complications described as "bilious cholera."

Presidential Term: March 5, 1849–July 9, 1850

Age at Inauguration: 64 years, 100 days

Vice President: Millard Fillmore

Married: Margaret Mackall Smith on June 21, 1810

Children: Ann Mackall Taylor, Sarah Knox Taylor, Octavia P. Taylor, Margaret Smith Taylor, Mary Elizabeth Taylor, Richard Taylor

Religion: Episcopalian

Education: No formal education

Occupation: Soldier

ZACHARY TAYLOR did not learn of his June 1848 nomination as the Whig candidate for the presidency until a month later because the letter informing him of this decision arrived at his home with ten cents postage due and he wouldn't pay it. He received lots of mail due to his successes in the Mexican-American War and many letters came with postage due. He refused them all and was reportedly somewhat embarrassed when he learned precisely which letter was included in the batch.

When Taylor was elected president in 1849, the sixty-four-year-old cavalry general had never voted.

Taylor rode his horse sidesaddle, even in battle.

Taylor had a canary named Johnny Ty. Deciding it was time for Johnny to have a mate, he brought another canary into his cage. Johnny Ty was found dead shortly thereafter. Turns out the mate had been another male.

Taylor was the first U.S. president who was ever elected without having ever served in any elected office.

Taylor would spit tobacco juice on the White House rugs if a spittoon wasn't in spitting distance.

Taylor's nicknames included Old Rough and Ready, and Zach.

On occasion, Taylor stuttered.

What James Polk said about Taylor: "He is evidently a weak man and has been made giddy with the idea of the Presidency."

Taylor used slaves as servants in the White House. He housed them in the attic.

Taylor and James Madison were second cousins.

Confederate president Jefferson Davis was Taylor's son-in-law.

Taylor died from gastroenteritis brought on by eating a large bowl of cherries and chasing it with a pitcher of iced milk. Why would he consume such a gastronomic abomination? He was hot and he believed that the cherries and milk would cool him. It is not known if he felt cooler before they killed him. Taylor attended Fourth of July festivities under a blazing sun heavily dressed, followed by a walk in the direct sun, and then ate the aforementioned cherries and iced milk, both of which were dangerous to eat in Washington during the summer due to the city's inadequate food sanitation capabilities. Taylor developed terrible cramps, and over the next few days suffered from severe diarrhea, vomiting, and coughing up of green bile. His doctors' diagnoses included cholera morbus, bilious fever, and typhoid fever. Taylor's body could not take the repeated and relentless assault on his bodily systems and he died on July 9, five days after his day in the sun.

Taylor's last words were "I am about to die. I expect the summons very soon. I have tried to discharge my duties faithfully. I regret nothing, but I am sorry that I am about to leave my friends."

Taylor's eulogy was given by Abraham Lincoln.

In the late 1980s, a college professor named Clara Rising put forth the suspicion that Taylor was murdered by poison. Was our twelfth president actually assassinated? Rising persuaded Taylor's closest relative to approve an exhumation and postmortem testing. The results were conclusive that Taylor was not poisoned but did in fact die of acute gastroenteritis. Rising ultimately self-published a book called *The Taylor File* in which she wrote about Taylor's "mysterious death," although after the exhumation and postmortem testing, it seems pretty obvious that there was no mystery at all regarding his death.

In 2009, the U.S. Mint released the Taylor $1 presidential coin. His portrait was on the front of the coin, the Statue of Liberty on the reverse side. Taylor had previously been commemorated on a U.S. quarter.

Taylor has been played in movies by Allan Cavan and James Gammon.

CHAPTER THIRTEEN

MILLARD FILLMORE

1850–1853 (Whig)

Born: January 7, 1800

Died: March 8, 1874

Cause of Death: Stroke.

Presidential Term: July 9, 1850–March 3, 1853

Age at Inauguration: 50 years, 183 days

Vice President: None. (At the time, there was no Constitutional mechanism to replace a vice president who ascended to the presidency, thus the position remained vacant.)

Married: Abigail Powers on February 5, 1826; Caroline Carmichael McIntosh on February 10, 1858

Children: Millard Powers Fillmore, Mary Abigail Fillmore

Religion: Unitarian

Education: No formal education

Occupation: Lawyer

Presidents **MILLARD FILLMORE** and Andrew Johnson were both slaves when they were young boys. Actually, the term used was *indentured servant* but the reality was that indentured servants were little more than slaves who had to buy their freedom to be let go.

★

Fillmore married his high school teacher.

★

Fillmore's favorite color was fuchsia.

★

Fillmore was particularly solicitous of his health, almost to the point of being a fanatic. He was known to leave Washington and travel to Georgetown to sleep when it was sweltering in the capital to prevent the chance of contracting malaria.

★

The first book Fillmore ever owned was a dictionary. He bought it with his own money.

★

Fillmore was the first U.S. president to establish a library in the White House.

Fillmore is known for this quote: "An honorable defeat is better than a dishonorable victory. This may be true of sports but in the affairs of Nations, it is not applicable." It's interesting that the second sentence of this quote is often not cited when attributing it to Fillmore.

Fillmore's wife Abigail had the first bathtub with running water installed in the White House.

In 1858, widower Fillmore signed a prenup before marrying Caroline McIntosh (thirteen years younger than he), the wealthy widow of a railroad magnate.

What Harry Truman said about Fillmore: "[W]hen we needed a strong man, what we got was a man that swayed with the slightest breeze."

Fillmore's nicknames included the American Louis Philippe and His Accidency.

Fillmore believed that slavery was protected by the U.S. Constitution.

Fillmore's son, Millard Powers Fillmore, burned his father's papers after his death. It is believed that this has contributed to a relatively negative assessment of Fillmore as a president. The American public's inability to assess a president's own words in his own writings tends to result in assuming the worst. It seems that when the administration's doings are all that remains, historians cannot fully appraise the true nature of a president. Harry Truman commented on the burning of Fillmore's papers in his book *Mr. Citizen*: "No papers or letters of a President should be destroyed, for none is too trivial or too personal but that it reveals something to future historians of a President's character and thoughts."

Fillmore has been played in movies by Millard Vincent.

CHAPTER FOURTEEN

FRANKLIN PIERCE

1853–1857 (Democrat)

Born: November 23, 1804

Died: October 8, 1869

Cause of Death: Complications and heart failure caused by chronic, severe inflammation of the stomach from years of alcohol abuse, compounded by dropsy, an accumulation of lymph in tissues and body cavities.

Presidential Term: March 4, 1853–March 3, 1857

Age at Inauguration: 48 years, 101 days

Vice President: William R. King

Married: Jane Means Appleton on November 19, 1834

Children: Franklin Pierce, Frank Robert Pierce, Benjamin Pierce

Religion: Episcopalian

Education: Bowdoin College, graduated 1824

Occupation: Lawyer, public official

When he was a kid, **FRANKLIN PIERCE** fell into a river and almost drowned . . . on Election Day.

★

One of Pierce's typical reactions to a confrontation was to faint. Often, several times.

★

Pierce's official 1852 campaign slogan was "We Polked you in '44, we shall Pierce you in '52."

★

Pierce and his wife both had tuberculosis and spit up blood.

★

Even though Pierce was the first president to have a full-time bodyguard, he was still attacked when he was in office. A deranged man threw a hard-boiled egg at him. When caught, the egg-sassin tried to kill himself with a pocketknife. Pierce didn't press charges.

★

Pierce's nicknames included the Fainting President, Young Hickory of the Granite Hills, and Handsome Frank.

Pierce's inaugural address was 3,319 words long. He memorized the entire speech and delivered it without notes. Today, that would be the equivalent of more than thirteen typed, double-spaced pages. Now, that's impressive.

What did Pierce describe as "the unshaken rock"? The U.S. Constitution.

Pierce was the only president to refuse to say "I solemnly swear" when he was sworn in as president. He instead said "I solemnly affirm." He also refused to swear his oath on a Bible. He used a law book instead.

What Theodore Roosevelt said about Pierce: "[He is a] small politician, of low capacity and mean surroundings, proud to act as the servile tool of men worse than himself but also stronger and abler. He was ever ready to do any work the slavery leaders set to him."

Pierce ran over a woman with his horse while he was president and was arrested. They let him go when they realized he was the president.

Pierce was with American author Nathaniel Hawthorne on a canoeing trip when Hawthorne died in his sleep.

Pierce was the first president to put up a Christmas tree in the White House.

Pierce was almost certainly an alcoholic, but from all accounts he went on the wagon during his presidential term.

The campaign slogan Pierce's own party came up with when Pierce was hoping to run for a second term: "Anybody but Pierce." Pierce's reaction when he wasn't nominated? "There's nothing left . . . but to get drunk."

Pierce has been played in a movie by Porter Hall.

CHAPTER FIFTEEN

JAMES BUCHANAN

1857–1861 (Democrat)

Born: April 23, 1791

Died: June 1, 1868

Cause of Death: Pneumonia and pericarditis (inflammation of the lining of the heart) caused by chronic rheumatic gout and chronic dysentery, both of which severely compromised his immune system.

Presidential Term: March 4, 1857–March 3, 1861

Age at Inauguration: 65 years, 315 days

Vice President: John C. Breckinridge

Married: Never married

Children: None

Religion: Presbyterian

Education: Dickinson College, graduated 1809

Occupation: Lawyer

JAMES BUCHANAN was the only American president to remain a bachelor his entire life. His niece Harriet Lane served as White House hostess during his administration.

The aforementioned Ms. Lane was more popular than her president uncle. The song "Listen to the Mocking Bird" was dedicated to her.

Buchanan was nearsighted in one eye and farsighted in the other. Thus to compensate for this visual weakness, he would constantly open and close one eye at a time, depending on whether he needed to see close or far. He would also cock his head on an angle to compensate for his bizarre ocular condition.

Buchanan's nicknames included the Bachelor President, Old Buck, the Old Public Functionary, the Sage of Wheatland, Ten-Cent Jimmy, and the Squire.

Buchanan, the only never-married president, had a twenty-three-year friendship with the only never-married vice president (under Franklin Pierce) William Rufus King. Buchanan and King were referred to "Miss Nancy and Aunt Fancy." King was also commonly described as "Mrs. Buchanan." So was Buchanan the only gay president? He was probably bisexual, since his letters also talk about his romances with women. A quote that seems to support the contention that he was gay is, "I am now 'solitary and alone,' having no companion in the house with me. I have gone a wooing to several gentlemen, but have not succeeded with any one of them. I feel that it is not good for man to be alone, and [I] should not be astonished to find myself married to some old maid who can nurse me when I am sick, provide good dinners for me when I am well, and not expect from me any very ardent or romantic affection."

Buchanan was a big boozer. During a serious imbibing session, he would start with cognac and ultimately end up drinking rye. According to historians, he'd easily consume two to three bottles at one sitting and he reportedly had what's been humorously described as a "wooden (empty) leg" and never ended up with a hangover. He did suffer from gout, though, a common affliction for the serious drinker.

On most Sundays, Buchanan would go for ride, during which he'd make a stop at his favorite distillery and pick up a ten-gallon barrel of Old J. B. Whiskey. This would be for the week and be in addition to whatever other adult beverages he had delivered to the White House for his imbibing pleasure.

Buchanan sent the very first presidential trans-Atlantic telegram. It was a greeting to Queen Victoria of Great Britain.

Texas senator Louis Wigfall plotted to kidnap Buchanan and install Vice President John C. Breckinridge in his place.

Buchanan regularly purchased slaves in Washington, D.C., and then sent them to Pennsylvania where they were freed.

Buchanan was what we would today call a pain in the neck. He would intercept his niece's mail, open it, read it, and then reseal it and write "Opened by mistake" on the envelope. He nitpicked, complained, micromanaged, and was generally annoying to those around him. Good thing he never married.

What Ulysses S. Grant said about Buchanan: "[Buchanan is] our present granny executive."

As president, Buchanan enjoyed hosting sauerkraut and mashed potato parties.

Buchanan had an eagle and an elephant as pets.

Buchanan has never been played in a movie.

CHAPTER SIXTEEN

ABRAHAM LINCOLN

1861–1865 (Republican)

Born: February 12, 1809

Died: April 15 1865

Cause of Death: Assassinated. Lincoln was shot in the head on April 14, 1865, and never regained consciousness. He died the following day.

Presidential Term: March 4, 1861–April 15, 1865

Age at Inauguration: 52 years, 20 days

Vice Presidents: Hannibal Hamlin, Andrew Johnson

Married: Mary Todd on November 4, 1842

Children: Robert Todd Lincoln, Edward Baker Lincoln, William "Willie" Wallace Lincoln, Thomas "Tad" Lincoln

Religion: No formal affiliation

Education: No formal education

Occupation: Lawyer

When **ABRAHAM LINCOLN** was nine, a horse kicked him in the forehead while he was in the middle of a sentence. He fell unconscious for several hours and when he awoke, his first words were the completion of the sentence he had been saying when the horse kicked him.

Lincoln was a licensed bartender. He owned a saloon before becoming president.

Lincoln and John Wilkes Booth were photographed together at Lincoln's inauguration.

A Union captain once sent Lincoln a mail-order ad for pornographic pictures. Captain M. G. Tousley was extremely upset that soldiers were buying and passing around pictures of naked girls, including series titled "Indian Maidens," "Wood Nymphs' Frolic," and "Circassian Slavegirls." Self-appointed censor of military morality Tousley wanted his president to know that Union soldiers were—*gasp!*—looking at dirty pictures.

During the Lincoln administration, one third of the U.S. currency was counterfeit. Why? Because sixteen hundred state banks issued currency and there was no uniform federal design for money. We can't help but wonder if the Constitution's "Full Faith and Credit" clause worked when it came to money.

That tall, black stovepipe hat that Lincoln used to wear was much more than just a hat. Lincoln used it as a portable filing cabinet and kept notes, money, and letters in it.

Lincoln had syphilis sometime around 1835–1836. His law partner William Herndon reported this and historians have accepted the story as true.

In 1841, Lincoln had a tooth pulled—without anesthesia. The dentist took part of Lincoln's jaw with the tooth. When he needed another extraction in 1862 when he was president, he brought his own canister of chloroform with him.

When Lincoln's son Willie died in 1862, Lincoln refused to sign any presidential papers or documents for four days.

In 1863, fans of the president sent him a turkey for the Lincoln Thanksgiving table. Lincoln's young son Tad named it Jack and quickly embraced it as a pet. However, it was supposed to be dinner and the White House cook took Jack away from Tad with the intent of killing it and then, of course, cooking it. Tad burst into a Cabinet meeting crying. Lincoln stopped the meeting and took the time to write an official reprieve, thus sparing Jack the fate of being eaten. Aren't fathers great? This incident is believed to be the first official "pardoning" of a turkey by a U.S. president.

There is a high probability that in his final years Lincoln had cancer of the adrenal glands.

In late 1863 and early 1864, Lincoln had smallpox.

Lincoln could be considered a victim of domestic abuse. His wife, Mary, struck him several times during their marriage. Once she whacked him in the nose with a piece of wood while he read the paper. Another time she punched him in the face and was known to throw things at him. She even once ripped out a piece of his beard.

Lincoln's 1864 presidential campaign slogans were "Don't swap horses in midstream," and "Vote yourself a farm."

After Richmond fell during the Civil War, one black woman knelt before Lincoln during his visit to the city, and another told her son that a touch of Lincoln's clothes would eliminate his pain.

Social reformer and writer Frederick Douglass was refused entrance to the White House on the day of Lincoln's 1865 inauguration because he was black. Lincoln was horrified and immediately ordered that Douglass be let in as his invited guest. Because he had, indeed, invited him. He asked Douglass what he thought of his inaugural address, telling him, "There is no man in the country whose opinion I value more than yours."

Lincoln once left the stage during a political rally because he spotted one of his supporters being beaten. He picked up the assailant by his trousers and physically hurled him twelve feet away.

One of Lincoln's most memorable quotes on slavery was, "Whenever I hear anyone arguing for slavery, I feel a strong impulse to have it tried on him personally."

Lincoln's second inaugural address includes what might be his most memorable line, if not surpassing the Gettysburg Address, at the very least equaling it:

> With malice toward none, with charity for all, with firmness in the right as God gives us to see the right, let us strive on to finish the work we are in, to bind up the nation's wounds, to care for him who shall have borne the battle and for his widow and his orphan, to do all which may achieve and cherish a just and lasting peace among ourselves and with all nations.

Lincoln (and many other presidents, of course) was constantly besieged by people wanting something: a government job, a foreign ambassadorship, a bridge for back home, and so forth. Lincoln often told the story of a man who would not stop soliciting him for a foreign minister assignment. The man was relentless in his hectoring of Lincoln, but the repeated turndowns finally forced him to (probably reluctantly) acquiesce to accepting somewhat lesser largesse from Lincoln—an old pair of pants.

Lincoln's nicknames included the Ancient, the Emancipation President, Father Abraham, the Great Emancipator, Greatheart, Honest Abe, the Illinois Baboon, Old Abe, the Railsplitter, the Sage of Springfield, and the Sectional President.

There's no indication that Lincoln ever slept in the Lincoln bed. People historians are certain did sleep in it (aside from the guests who have stayed in the Lincoln Bedroom over the years) include Theodore and Edith Roosevelt, Woodrow and Edith Wilson, Calvin and Grace Coolidge, and Anna Roosevelt Boettiger, her husband John, and their son, Johnny.

Mary Todd Lincoln was extremely jealous and had no qualms about humiliating her husband the president in public. She couldn't stand other women giving Lincoln any attention whatsoever. After the Civil War, Mary accompanied her husband to a troop review in Virginia. These were done on horseback, and at one point, a woman rode next to Lincoln. Mary started shrieking at the woman and making a full-blown spectacle of herself, while completely mortifying her husband.

Lincoln was the classic definition of a raconteur, someone who tells stories in an entertaining or interesting way. When speaking with people one-on-one or in small groups, he would frequently intersperse his conversation with anecdotes, tall stories, and jokes.

Lincoln had, and would employ when necessary, what has been described as a "frontier" accent, saying, for example, "git" for "get."

During the Civil War, a temperance committee visited Lincoln at the White House and demanded that he immediately fire General Ulysses S. Grant. Why? Because he drinks, the president was told. Lincoln then made what might be one of his most famous statements ever: "I wish some of you would tell me the brand of whisky that General Grant drinks. I would like to send a barrel of it to every one of my other generals."

Lincoln hated the nickname "Abe" and no one who knew him ever dared to call him that to his face. Even his wife, Mary, addressed him as "Mr. Lincoln," or "Father."

Lincoln liked to be photographed.

Lincoln could recite flawlessly entire soliloquies from *Hamlet* and *Macbeth*.

When 307 Sioux Indians were arrested for a murderous attack on white settlements, Lincoln pardoned all but thirty-eight of them. Those thirty-eight, though, were summarily hung in the biggest mass execution in U.S. history.

Lincoln wrote poetry. Here is the text of one of his surviving poems, "My Childhood's Home I See Again." It's a poignant remembrance of going home.

My childhood's home I see again,
And sadden with the view;
And still, as memory crowds my brain,
There's pleasure in it too.
O Memory! thou midway world
'Twixt earth and paradise,
Where things decayed and loved ones lost
In dreamy shadows rise,
And, freed from all that's earthly vile,
Seem hallowed, pure, and bright,
Like scenes in some enchanted isle
All bathed in liquid light.
As dusky mountains please the eye
When twilight chases day;
As bugle-tones that, passing by,
In distance die away;
As leaving some grand waterfall,
We, lingering, list its roar—
So memory will hallow all
We've known, but know no more.
Near twenty years have passed away
Since here I bid farewell
To woods and fields, and scenes of play,
And playmates loved so well.
Where many were, but few remain
Of old familiar things;
But seeing them, to mind again
The lost and absent brings.
The friends I left that parting day,
How changed, as time has sped!

Young childhood grown, strong manhood gray,
And half of all are dead.
I hear the loved survivors tell
How nought from death could save,
Till every sound appears a knell,
And every spot a grave.
I range the fields with pensive tread,
And pace the hollow rooms,
And feel (companion of the dead)
I'm living in the tombs.

Lincoln was an official inventor. He received U.S. Patent No. 6469 in May 1849 for a device that would lift boats over shoals. His invention was never built and put into use, though.

Lincoln's Gettysburg Address is considered one of the finest pieces of oratory every written. In a mere 272 words, Lincoln established a national tone that would guide the country for decades. Yet not everyone liked it upon hearing it for the first time. The *Chicago Times* said, "The cheek of every American must tingle with shame as he reads the silly, flat and dishwatery utterances of the man who has to be pointed out to intelligent foreigners as the President of the United States." Ouch.

When Abe and Mary's son Willie Lincoln died in 1862 at the age of twelve, Mary was bereft beyond imagination. She held séances and hired spiritualists to make contact with her dead son. She also reported that he visited her every evening and would stand at the foot of her bed. In a letter to her sister she wrote, "He comes to me every night and stands at the foot of my bed with the same, sweet adorable smile." The president is reported to have attended some of his wife's séances.

Lincoln grew a beard because an eleven-year-old girl asked him to. Her name was Grace Bedell and she wrote the following letter:

Hon A B Lincoln . . .

Dear Sir

My father has just home from the fair and brought home your picture and Mr. Hamlin's. I am a little girl only 11 years old, but want you should be President of the United States very much so I hope you wont think me very bold to write to such a great man as you are. Have you any little girls about as large as I am if so give them my love and tell her to write to me if you cannot answer this letter. I have got 4 brothers and part of them will vote for you any way and if you let your whiskers grow I will try and get the rest of them to vote for you would look a great deal better for your face is so thin. All the ladies like whiskers and they would tease their husbands to vote for you and then you would be President. My father is going to vote for you and if I was a man I would vote for you to but I will try to get every one to vote for you that I can I think that rail fence around your picture makes it look very pretty I have got a little baby sister she is nine weeks old and is just as cunning as can be. When you direct your letter direct to Grace Bedell Westfield Chautauqua County New York.

I must not write any more answer this letter right off Good bye

Grace Bedell

Lincoln was quite bemused by this precocious young lady and wrote back to her four days later:

Springfield, Ill Oct 19, 1860
Miss Grace Bedell

My dear little Miss

Your very agreeable letter of the 15th is received—I regret the necessity of saying I have no daughters—I have three sons—one seventeen, one nine, and one seven years of age—They, with their mother, constitute my whole family—As to the whiskers, having never worn any, do you not think people would call it a piece of silly affectation if I were to begin it now?

Your very sincere well wisher

A. Lincoln

Lincoln's son Robert Todd was saved from injury or possibly death by Edwin Booth, the brother of his father's assassin John Wilkes Booth. In late 1864 or early 1865, Robert Todd lost his footing on a train platform in Jersey City, New Jersey. He was saved from falling under the suddenly moving train by Edwin Booth, who grabbed him by the collar and pulled him to safety.

It is believed that Lincoln manifested symptoms during adulthood suggesting heart disease, which would have been a result of his Marfan's syndrome. He frequently complained of involuntary movement of extremities, cold hands and feet, and fatigue and headaches. He was likely suffering from advanced heart disease at the time of his assassination.

Lincoln's last official act was to create the Department of the Treasury which, of course, oversees the Secret Service. (Too little, and a little too late, eh?)

John Wilkes Booth carried two pistols with him the night he assassinated Lincoln. He wanted to be certain of being able to kill him if the first gun didn't fire or he missed and he didn't have time to reload.

The third, fourth, and fifth cervical (neck) vertebrae of John Wilkes Booth are preserved at the National Museum of Health and Medicine.

After Lincoln's death, "fans" descended on the White House and walked off with twenty-two grand worth of china.

Thomas Corbett is known as Lincoln's Avenger because he was the soldier who shot Lincoln's assassin, John Wilkes Booth. Thomas Corbett, however, was off-the-wall crazy. He was a religious zealot, wore his hair like Jesus, and he castrated himself with a scissors because he feared he'd indulge in prostitutes. He got a job as a doorman at the Kansas House of Representatives and one day pulled a gun because he thought a prayer was being mocked. He ended up in an insane asylum, escaped, and is believed to have died in the Great Hinckley Fire of 1894. Corbett was a living manifestation of the expression "mad as a hatter." He had once worked as a hatter and the fumes from the mercury used in the manufacturing process are believed to have made him go crazy.

After his death, only Lincoln's head was autopsied.

Before Lincoln's body reached its final resting place in Memorial Hall in the Oak Ridge Cemetery in Springfield, Illinois, his coffin was moved seventeen times and opened six times.

Once, when Winston Churchill was a White House guest, he refused to stay overnight in the Lincoln Bedroom. He claimed he saw the ghost of Lincoln "lurking about" and wouldn't stay in a room that bore his name.

Lincoln has been played in movies by Joseph Henabery, J. Herbert Frank, George A. Billings Sr., Frank McGlynn Sr. (three times), John Carradine, Walter Huston, Henry Fonda, Raymond Massey (twice), John Anderson (twice), F. Murray Abraham, Robert V. Barron, Jason Robards, Hal Holbrook, Lance Henriksen, Brendan Fraser, Tim Willett, and Gerald Bestrom.

CHAPTER SEVENTEEN

ANDREW JOHNSON

1865–1869 (Democrat/National Union)

Born: December 29, 1808

Died: July 31, 1875

Cause of Death: Two strokes; possibly complicated by contracting cholera a couple of years earlier. When Johnson suffered the first of the two strokes that eventually killed him, he refused to allow a doctor or clergyman to be called.

Presidential Term: April 15, 1865–March 3, 1869

Age at Inauguration: 56 years, 107 days

Vice President: None. (At the time, there was no Constitutional mechanism to replace a vice president who as-

cended to the presidency, thus the position remained vacant.)

Married: Eliza McCardle on May 17, 1827

Children: Martha Johnson, Charles Johnson, Mary Johnson, Robert Johnson, Andrew Johnson

Religion: No formal affiliation

Education: No formal education

Occupation: Tailor, public official

ANDREW JOHNSON was the only U.S. president not to have even one day of formal schooling. He taught himself how to read.

When, as a young man, Johnson moved his family to Tennessee, their cart was pulled by a blind pony.

Johnson was drunk at his inauguration as Lincoln's vice president. Lincoln was reportedly so embarrassed by Johnson's incoherent ramblings he hung his head in shame. How bad was it? Aside from Johnson going on for seventeen minutes instead of seven, he was also too drunk to swear in incoming senators. Clerks had to do it for him. Senator Zachariah Chandler later said,

> The inauguration went off very well except that the Vice President Elect was too drunk to perform his duties & disgraced himself & the Senate by making a drunken foolish speech. I was never so mortified in my life, had I been able to find a hole I would have dropped through it out of sight.

Johnson was against secession. And he said so. Virginians did not agree with him. When he arrived in that state to give a speech against secession, "concerned citizens" boarded his train, dragged him off, and beat the living crap out of him. They didn't hang him, though. They felt that privilege should be left for his native Tennesseans.

Johnson once claimed that God killed Lincoln so he, Johnson, could become president.

Johnson was an animal lover and left food out for the countless rats that infested the White House during his term.

Johnson was an avowed racist and slave owner and a confirmed white supremacist. After his elevation to president following Lincoln's assassination, Johnson said, "This is a country for white men, and by God, as long as I am president, it shall be a government for white men."

Johnson pardoned every former member of the Confederacy. All they had to do was pledge allegiance to the post–Civil War United States. Oh, and not have slaves, too.

Johnson's nicknames included the Daddy of the Baby, the Father of the Homestead, His Accidency, King Andy, and the Veto.

What Ulysses S. Grant said about Johnson: "I would impeach him because he is such an infernal liar."

Johnson was the only former U.S. president elected to the U.S. Senate after serving as president.

Johnson's pillow in his coffin was a copy of the U.S. Constitution.

Johnson has been played in movies by Van Heflin and Dennis Clark.

CHAPTER EIGHTEEN

ULYSSES S. GRANT

1869–1877 (Republican)

Born: April 27, 1822

Died: July 23, 1885

Cause of Death: Cancer of the tongue and throat. Grant's lifelong smoking habit caused the tongue and throat cancer that ultimately killed him. In his final days, the retired president became addicted to the cocaine that doctors were using to swab his throat and he needed regular morphine injections for the intractable pain.

Presidential Term: March 4, 1869–March 3, 1877

Age at Inauguration: 46 years, 311 days

Vice Presidents: Schuyler Colfax, Henry Wilson

Married: Julia Boggs Dent on August 22, 1848

Children: Frederick Dent Grant, Ulysses Simpson Grant, Ellen Wrenshall Grant, Jesse Root Grant

Religion: Methodist

Education: U.S. Military Academy at West Point, graduated 1843

Occupation: Soldier (general)

GRANT's real name was Hiram Ulysses Grant, but he so loathed his initials—HUG—that he began using Ulysses as his first name.

Ulysses S. Grant's father bestowed the nickname "Useless" on him. (Nothing like a little negative reinforcement to set a kid off on the right path, eh?)

Grant's initial life plan was to become a mathematics professor.

Grant's 1868 presidential campaign slogan was "Vote as you shot."

While president, Grant was once arrested for speeding—in his horse-drawn carriage. He insisted on paying the fine and wrote a letter to the cop's boss complimenting the officer on his respect for the law—regardless of who the lawbreaker was!

Canaries were supposed to sing at Grant's inauguration. However, it was so cold that day that they all froze to death before singing a note.

His hard-drinking, war hero rep notwithstanding, Grant did not like profanity or off-colored stories.

Grant's nicknames included the Butcher from Galena, the Great Hammerer, the Hero of Appomattox, Hug Grant, Lyss, the Man on Horseback, Old Three Stars, Texas, Uncle Sam, Unconditional Surrender, the Uniformed Soldier, United States, and Useless.

Grant ate his meat cooked black.

Grant's wife, Julia, was cross-eyed from birth and would sometimes walk sideways to avoid crashing into people. Or furniture. Or walls.

Grant never let anyone see him naked. Except maybe his wife. On the battlefield, soldiers bathed by stripping down and having their comrades-in-arms pour water over them. Not Grant. He hid in a sealed tent so no one could see him.

After a successful Civil War battle, appreciative American citizens sent Grant ten thousand boxes of cigars. If each box held twenty-five cigars, that comes to a staggering quarter of a million cigars Grant would ultimately smoke. (No wonder he died of throat cancer.)

The sight of blood made Grant nauseous.

We all know the riddle, "Who is buried in Grant's Tomb?" Groucho Marx came up with this for his game show *You Bet Your Life* so that everyone could win at least something on the show. He'd always accept "Grant" as a correct answer but the truth is that Grant is not *buried* in Grant's Tomb. He's *entombed* there.

Grant's favorite breakfast was cucumbers in vinegar.

Grant smoked up to twenty cigars a day from a young age, and the habit eventually killed him after he developed cancer of the throat in 1884. He refused to succumb to the disease, however, until he completed the writing of his autobiography, *Personal Memoirs of U. S. Grant* (two volumes, 1885–1886), a tome that is now considered a literary masterpiece. There may be good reason why the two-volume epic is held in such high regard: If it wasn't actually ghostwritten by Mark Twain, it is at least believed that Twain did an editorial polish. Regardless of whether he did the hands-on writing, Twain considered Grant's *Memoirs* "a great, unique and unapproachable literary masterpiece. There is no higher literature than these modest, simple Memoirs. Their style is at least flawless, and no man can improve upon it."

Grant's last word was "Water."

Grant has been played in movies by Joseph Crehan, Jason Robards, and Kevin Kline.

CHAPTER NINETEEN

RUTHERFORD B. HAYES

1877–1881 (Republican)

Born: October 4, 1822

Died: January 17, 1893

Cause of Death: Heart failure. As was the case with President Harrison, Hayes's death may have been hastened by his catching a cold and refusing to rest.

Presidential Term: March 4, 1877–March 3, 1881

Age at Inauguration: 54 years, 151 days

Vice President: William A. Wheeler

Married: Lucy Ware Webb on December 30, 1852

Children: Birchard Austin Hayes, James Webb Cook Hayes, Rutherford Platt Hayes, Joseph Thompson Hayes, George

Crook Hayes, Fanny Hayes, Scott Russell Hayes, Manning Force Hayes

Religion: No formal affiliation, but he attended a Methodist church with his wife

Education: Kenyon College, graduated 1842; Harvard Law School, graduated 1845

Occupation: Lawyer

When **RUTHERFORD B. HAYES** was young, he suffered lyssophobia. This is the fear of going insane.

★

Hayes lost the 1876 presidential election to Samuel Tilden by the popular vote (4,284,020–4,036,572). So how did Hayes become the nineteenth president of the United States? The electoral commission (forerunner of today's electoral college) "awarded" him twenty electoral votes, giving him a 185–184 win. As you might imagine, Tilden was pissed. (Did they say "pissed" back then? Regardless of historical usage, that's the word to describe Samuel Tilden's reaction to his loss.)

The Hayes White House was dry, thanks to Hayes's booze-loathing wife, who ended up nicknamed Lemonade Lucy after one particular incident. One day, the president squeezed a berry into a glass of lemonade. To his wife, the resultant beverage looked like wine. She went nuts and calmed down only after her husband explained he had not fallen off the wagon. The press found out about this skirmish, and she was immediately dubbed Lemonade Lucy. (After attending a dinner at the Hayes White House, Secretary of State William Evarts once remarked "Water flowed like champagne!")

Hayes and his family spent every evening in the White House singing hymns.

The first phone in the White House was installed during Hayes's term. The "installer" was Alexander Graham Bell. (It's not known if Bell was on time for the service call and whether Hayes had to be home between eight and noon or one and five.)

Hayes is the only U.S. president to be sworn in to office inside the White House. However, there is a codicil to that historical fact. When Barack Obama was sworn in as president on January 20, 2009, the Supreme Court Chief Justice John Roberts screwed up the wording of the oath. The oath should read:

> I do solemnly swear (or affirm) that I will faithfully execute the Office of President of the United States, and will to the best of my ability, preserve, protect and defend the Constitution of the United States.

Chief Roberts recited the oath incorrectly by putting *faithfully* after "President of the United States." Obama hesitated and looked at the judge, who failed to correct his mistake. Obama then recited it the way Roberts had said it. This did not go over well with . . . well, with anyone, truth be told. So on the following day, Wednesday, January 21, 2009, Chief Justice Roberts, out of what he described as "an abundance of caution," re-administered the oath to by-then-president Obama as they both stood in the Oval Office. No one brought a Bible, and Obama took the oath without one. And as to why Hayes was sworn in at the White House, it was probably because the Republicans were afraid the Democrats would try to install

Tilden in as president. President Grant's term expired on a Sunday, and Hayes's inauguration wasn't scheduled until Monday. Thus Hayes was secretly sworn in on Sunday at the White House.

Hayes's nicknames included the Dark Horse, Granny Hayes, His Fraudulency, Old Eight-to-Seven, and President De Facto.

Hayes was the first U.S. president to have a typewriter in the White House. It was a manual, of course.

One of the privates who served in Hayes's regiment during the Civil War was future president William McKinley.

Hayes was the first president to get a presidential library. It was opened in 1916 and houses Hayes's twelve-thousand-volume library. It is part of the Rutherford B. Hayes Presidential Center in Fremont, Ohio. (The first presidential library in the National Archives system, however, was the Franklin D. Roosevelt Library in Hyde Park, New York, dedicated June 30, 1941.)

After his term as president, Hayes served as the president of the National Prison Association.

Hayes has been played in a movie by John Dilson.

CHAPTER TWENTY

JAMES A. GARFIELD

1881 (Republican)

Born: November 19, 1831

Died: September 19, 1881

Cause of Death: Assassinated. Garfield was shot on July 2, 1881, and after undergoing several surgeries performed with bare hands and unsterilized instruments, he died of blood poisoning a little over two months after being shot.

Presidential Term: March 4, 1881–September 19, 1881

Age at Inauguration: 49 years, 105 days

Vice President: Chester A. Arthur

Married: Lucretia Rudolph on November 11, 1858

Children: Eliza A. Garfield, Harry A. Garfield, James R. Garfield, Mary Garfield, Irvin M. Garfield, Abram Garfield, Edward Garfield

Religion: Disciples of Christ

Education: Western Reserve Eclectic Institute (now Hiram College), attended 1851–1854; Williams College, graduated 1856

Occupation: Teacher, public official

When **JAMES GARFIELD** was sixteen, he left home to work on barges and tugboats. He fell overboard fourteen times and ended up with malaria. He respectfully resigned his position.

Before he became president, Garfield wrote a proof of the Pythagorean theorem that was published in the *New England Journal of Education* and is still discussed in mathematics textbooks today. Rather than using squares to prove the theorem, Garfield's proof uses trapezoids.

Garfield could simultaneously write Greek with one hand and Latin with the other.

Garfield was the only ordained preacher ever to be elected president of the United States.

Garfield issued no presidential pardons during his administration.

Garfield's nicknames included the Canal Boy, the Martyr President, the Preacher, and the Teacher President.

What Ulysses S. Grant said about Garfield: "Garfield has shown that he is not possessed of the backbone of an angleworm."

Garfield was an accomplished Indian club juggler.

Garfield was a very touchy-feely kind of guy. He hugged, rubbed, and was an arm-around-the-shoulder talker.

Garfield's mother was the first mother of a president to attend her son's inauguration.

Garfield may have had a premonition of his own death. He reported routinely feeling a sense of foreboding after becoming president and, according to *The Complete Book of U.S. Presidents,* had dreams in which he "was naked and lost."

One of the earliest air-conditioning units was built to make the suffering Garfield more comfortable. As the president lay in bed in the sweltering Washington, D.C., heat with a bullet in him, navy engineers came up with a plan. They brought in six tons of ice and placed it in a container in the basement of the White House. They then rigged up a series of ducts and fans that blew cold air from the ice up into the president's bedroom. Amazingly, this contraption lowered the temperature of the room by twenty degrees.

After Garfield was shot, he was fed rectally. (You can write your own joke.)

The medical bill to treat James Garfield after he was shot totaled $18,500.

When Garfield was shot on July 2, 1881, one of his doctors was none other than Alexander Graham Bell. He had invented an electrical device he said would find the bullet in the president's body. It didn't. Garfield died of his wounds seventy-nine days later on September 19, 1881.

Garfield has been played in a movie by Francis Sayles.

CHAPTER TWENTY-ONE

CHESTER A. ARTHUR

1881–1885 (Republican)

Born: October 5, 1829

Died: November 18, 1886

Cause of Death: A stroke, probably caused by renal failure from Bright's disease, a fatal kidney ailment.

Presidential Term: September 19, 1881–March 3, 1885

Age at Inauguration: 51 years, 349 days

Vice President: None

Married: Ellen Lewis Herndon on October 25, 1859

Children: William Lewis Herndon Arthur, Chester Alan Arthur, Ellen Herndon Arthur

Religion: Episcopalian

Education: Union College, graduated 1848

Occupation: Lawyer

CHESTER A. ARTHUR was born in Fairfield, Vermont. When he was a child, however, his family moved to Canada. When he was running for vice president in 1880, his opponents lied about his place of birth and claimed that since he was "born in Canada," he was ineligible to be vice president. (Hmm. Nothing new under the sun, right?)

When Arthur was president, he had eighty pairs of pants. And he didn't just leave them in the closet, alternating a new pair for almost three months. He reportedly changed clothes throughout the day.

After being elected president, Arthur thought the White House was shabby and refused to live there until the building was completely remodeled.

Arthur once held an auction to raise money for better furnishings in the White House. Two of the things he auctioned off were Abraham Lincoln's pants and John Quincy Adams's hat.

Arthur was the only president to wear muttonchop whiskers.

Arthur was a dandy: a fashionable dresser who spent a lot of money on clothes and liked to look very put together. We also know that he changed clothes several times a day. (He did, after all, have at least the aforementioned eighty pairs of pants in his closet.)

Arthur's nicknames included Arthur the Gentleman, the Dude, the First Gentleman of the Land, His Accidency, Our Chet, and Prince Arthur.

What Woodrow Wilson said about Arthur: "[Arthur is] a non-entity with side whiskers."

Arthur had a picture in the White House of his beloved, deceased wife, Ellen. He ordered that fresh flowers be placed next to the photo every single day.

Something a president could never say today, but that Arthur did say: "I may be President of the United States, but my private life is nobody's damned business."

Arthur had Bright's disease, which is known today as the kidney disease chronic nephritis. He kept it a secret for his entire presidency.

Arthur, lying on his deathbed and worried about his place in American history, had all his papers and correspondence placed into a trash can and burned as he watched.

Arthur has been played in a movie by Emmett Corrigan.

CHAPTER TWENTY-TWO

GROVER CLEVELAND

1885–1889 (Democrat)

Born: March 18, 1837

Died: June 24, 1908

Cause of Death: Heart failure caused by complications from severe rheumatism, chronic nephritis, and chronic gastritis. In his final months, Cleveland used a pump on himself to drain his stomach in an attempt to get some relief from his crippling abdominal pains.

Presidential Terms: March 4, 1885–March 3, 1889; March 4, 1893–March 3, 1897

Age at Inauguration: 47 years, 351 days (1st term); 55 years, 351 days (2nd term)

Vice Presidents: Thomas A. Hendricks, Adlai E. Stevenson

Married: Frances Folsom on June 2, 1886

Children: Oscar Folsom Cleveland (alleged illegitimate child), Ruth Cleveland, Esther Cleveland, Marion Cleveland, Richard Folsom Cleveland, Francis Grover Cleveland

Religion: Presbyterian

Education: No formal education

Occupation: Lawyer

The title of this book comes from a little-known incident that occurred during the administration of our twenty-second (and twenty-fourth) president, **GROVER CLEVELAND**. In 1893, the heavy smoker was diagnosed as having a malignant tumor of the mouth. Fearing a financial panic that would make the current U.S. Depression (known as the Panic of 1893) worse, Cleveland's condition was not revealed to the public. Cleveland was secretly operated on aboard the yacht *Oneida* on the East River in New York on July 1, 1893, by five doctors and a dentist who removed his left upper jaw and a large tumor while he was strapped to a mast. The president was fitted with a rubber jaw and spent months learning how to speak naturally again. Cleveland's surgery was not revealed to the American public until 1917, twenty-four years after his operation.

Cleveland was a hangman. As sheriff of Erie County, New York, he took upon himself the duty of placing the hangman's noose around the necks of two criminals who had been sentenced to death.

Cleveland once avoided military service by paying a Polish immigrant $150 to take his place.

Cleveland was portly. His nickname was Uncle Jumbo.

Cleveland's favorite meal was corned beef and cabbage.

One of Cleveland's confidantes was Isidor Straus, who had the misfortune of going down with the *Titanic*. Straus's wife also died, not wanting to leave her husband's side.

One of Cleveland's 1884 presidential campaign slogans was "Blaine, Blaine, James G. Blaine. Continental Liar from the State of Maine."

Cleveland's nicknames included Big Beefhead, the Buffalo Hangman, the Claimant, the Dumb Prophet, His Accidency, the Man of Destiny, Old Grover, Old Veto, the People's President, the Perpetual Candidate, the Pretender, the Sage of Princeton, the Stuffed Prophet, and Uncle Jumbo.

Cleveland signed the law that made the first Monday in September an official holiday called Labor Day. It was intended to honor workers. Today it is seen as the unofficial end of summer and a very big day for retail sales.

The Baby Ruth candy bar was not named for Cleveland's daughter Ruth. It was named for Babe Ruth, but the candy company claimed it was named for the president's daughter so they could get out of paying the Babe royalties for use of his name.

Cleveland was known to personally answer the White House phone.

Cleveland was a veto machine. In his first term, he issued 414 vetoes, more than all his predecessors combined.

The U.S. Treasury once issued a $1,000 bill, and Grover Cleveland was on it.

Cleveland was Ulysses S. Grant's sixth cousin, once removed.

Ever hear of James E. King? He was a prominent Buffalo, New York, gynecologist who died in 1947. He was also believed to have been Cleveland's illegitimate son. Cleveland admitted to an affair with a woman named Maria Halpin, who was also having an affair with one of Cleveland's friends and his law partner, Oscar Folsom. When Halpin had a son, she named him Oscar Folsom Cleveland. She knew that either of the two men could have been the father, but she went after Cleveland for money. Cleveland did pay child support for the boy because he acknowledged that Oscar could have been his son. His opponents used the revelation of Oscar against Cleveland, but he won anyway. He instructed his staff to simply tell the truth: Yes, Cleveland had had an affair with Maria Halpin, and yes, he is paying support even though he is not certain Oscar is his son. Today, a simple paternity test would have put this to rest, but back then, a man's character determined how he would react in a situation such as this. The public believed Cleveland reacted properly. Oscar was eventually adopted into the James King family and became known as James E. King.

Cleveland was a duck hunter. He even named his gun Death and Destruction.

Cleveland's last words were "I have tried so hard to do right."

Cleveland has been played in movies by Stuart Holmes (twice) and Pat McCormick.

CHAPTER TWENTY-THREE

BENJAMIN HARRISON

1889–1893 (Republican)

Born: August 20, 1833

Died: March 13, 1901

Cause of Death: Pneumonia, caused by the flu. Harrison's doctors tried treating the retired president with inhalation therapy but he deteriorated and died a few weeks after contracting the flu.

Presidential Term: March 4, 1889–March 3, 1893

Age at Inauguration: 55 years, 196 days

Vice President: Levi P. Morton

Married: Caroline Lavinia Scott on October 20, 1853; Mary Scott Lord Dimmick on April 6, 1896

Children: Russell Benjamin Harrison, Mary Scott Harrison, Elizabeth Harrison

Religion: Presbyterian

Education: Miami University of Ohio, graduated 1852

Occupation: Lawyer

BENJAMIN HARRISON's great-grandfather signed the Declaration of Independence, and his grandfather was President William Henry Harrison. Some lineage, eh?

During Harrison's time in the White House, electric lights were installed for the first time. Harrison was terrified of the light switches and thought that he would be zapped with electric shocks if he touched them. Thus he left all the lights in the White House on all night long, rather than turn them off and risk electrocution. The White House electrician would have to turn them off when he arrived for work in the morning.

Harrison was the last bearded president.

During his administration, Harrison pardoned all the Mormons who had previously engaged in plural marriage. (Think he'd be a *Big Love* fan?)

Harrison once chased a goat-driven cart down Pennsylvania Avenue when the goat, Old Whiskers, took off with Harrison's grandchildren in the cart.

One of Harrison's nicknames was the Human Iceberg, and it wasn't because he had cold hands and feet. He was, shall we say, a less than friendly and warm person. He was a social dud with the interpersonal and communication skills of a large rock. (Yes, that's documented.)

Harrison was the first president to attend a baseball game. The Cincinnati Reds beat the Washington Senators 7–4 on Monday, June 6, 1892.

Harrison's other nicknames included Baby McKee's Grandfather, Chinese Harrison, the Grandfather's Hat, Kid Gloves, and Little Ben.

Washington, D.C., is downstream from Johnston, Pennsylvania. When the devastating Johnston Flood occurred in 1889 during Harrison's administration, the Capitol was flooded with diluted sewage.

Harrison was president when North Dakota and South Dakota were admitted to the Union. It seems that the two states had a powerful case of sibling rivalry, so in order to not play favorites Harrison had the state names on the paperwork hidden from his sight so no one would know which statehood document he signed first. You'd think this would have placated the two states, but no such luck. When the official paperwork was filed, it was done alphabetically; thus North Dakota won the title of thirty-ninth state and South Dakota had to settle with being number forty.

Harrison was the first president to have his voice recorded. His words were recorded on an Edison wax cylinder around 1889. He said, "As President of the United States, I was present at the first Pan-American Congress in Washington, D.C. I believe that with God's help, our two countries shall continue to live side-by-side, in peace and prosperity. Benjamin Harrison."

Harrison once gave 140 completely different speeches over a period of a single month. That's almost five original speeches a day.

Harrison's was the first Congress to spend more than $1 billion. This happened during Harrison's first two years in office, and once the country hit that mark it never went back.

Harrison has been played in a movie by Roy Gordon.

CHAPTER TWENTY-FOUR

GROVER CLEVELAND

1893–1897 (Democrat)

See Chapter 22.

CHAPTER TWENTY-FIVE

WILLIAM MCKINLEY

1897–1901 (Republican)

Born: January 29, 1843

Died: September 14, 1901

Cause of Death: Assassinated. McKinley was shot in the pancreas on September 6, 1901, and died eight days later from systemic failure caused by gangrene from the infected bullet wounds and bullet path.

Presidential Term: March 4, 1897–September 14, 1901

Age at Inauguration: 54 years, 34 days

Vice Presidents: Garret A. Hobart, Theodore Roosevelt

Married: Ida Saxton on January 25, 1871

Children: Katherine McKinley, Ida McKinley

Religion: Methodist

Education: Allegheny College (attended 1860–1861)

Occupation: Lawyer

WILLIAM MCKINLEY's 1896 presidential campaign slogan was "Patriotism, Protection, and Prosperity." His 1900 presidential campaign slogans were "Let Well Enough Alone" and "Four More Years of the Full Dinner Pail."

McKinley's wife, Ida, was an epileptic prone to frequent seizures, oftentimes in public. When that happened, announced by a strange, hissing sound emanating from her, her husband would drape a handkerchief over her face until the seizure stopped.

What Theodore Roosevelt said about McKinley: "McKinley has no more backbone than a chocolate éclair."

Supposedly, McKinley was Frank Baum's inspiration and model for the character of the Wizard of Oz.

McKinley's nicknames included the Idol of Ohio, the Napoleon of Protection, Prosperity's Advance Agent, the Stocking-Foot Orator, and Wobbly Willie.

Ida McKinley crocheted thirty-five hundred pairs of house slippers when her husband was president. They came in two colors, blue and gray. Yes, some were for Northerners, and some were for Confederates.

McKinley annexed the Hawaiian Islands in 1898 during his administration. This was the first step to statehood. Of his decision he said, "We need Hawaii just as much and a good deal more than we did California. It is manifest destiny." He also annexed Guam and Puerto Rico during his term.

The U.S. Treasury once issued a $500 bill, and McKinley was on it.

In the book *Presidential Anecdotes,* a story is told of McKinley's famous handshake:

> McKinley's handshake was famous. To save wear and tear on his right hand at receptions, the President developed what came to be called the "McKinley grip." In receiving lines, he would smile as a man came by, take his right hand and squeeze it warmly before his own hand got caught in a hard grip, hold the man's elbow with his left hand, and then swiftly pull him along and be ready to beam on the next guest.

McKinley could shake twenty-five hundred hands per hour. This is believed to be a presidential record. This is around forty handshakes a minute, or one every 1.5 seconds.

Ida McKinley single-handedly caused a bird to become an endangered species. She liked wearing a feathery boa that was made from the feathers of egrets. Because she was the First

Lady, her fashion choices quickly became a national obsession. So many egrets were plucked (and killed) to satisfy the demand for their feathers, they were declared an endangered species. Some of the egret (heron) species have made a comeback, but many are still endangered to this day.

McKinley was the last president who had fought in the Civil War.

Shortly before he was shot in 1901, McKinley had been offered a brand-new invention: a bulletproof vest. His secretary told the inventor the president was away and would consider it upon his return. McKinley was at the Pan-American Exposition in Buffalo, New York . . . where he got shot and died eight days later.

After McKinley was shot, he emphasized to his aides that they be very careful as to how they broke the news to his wife, Ida. Upon hearing what happened, Ida never again set foot in the White House. She also did not attend his burial.

Compared to some of the other presidents on their deathbeds, McKinley was remarkably composed and his sentiments spiritually elevated, as evidenced by his last words. Moments before his death on the afternoon of September 6, 1901, he said to those assembled, "Good-bye. Good-bye to all. It is God's will. His will, not ours, be done."

Today, the average time a death row inmate spends awaiting execution is fifteen years, and the time from sentencing to execution can sometimes run as long as twenty years. Times have certainly changed. McKinley's assassin, Leon Czolgosz, was executed in New York in the electric chair on October 29, 1901, for the assassination of McKinley, a mere forty-five days after the president's death on September 14. Is it true that there is a film of his electrocution? Not really, although there does exist a reenactment film of the execution done by Thomas Edison.

McKinley has been played in a movie by Brian Keith.

CHAPTER TWENTY-SIX

THEODORE ROOSEVELT

1901–1909 (Republican)

Born: October 27, 1858

Died: January 6, 1919

Cause of Death: Coronary embolism, complicated by chronic inflammatory rheumatism and recurring infections, including leg and ear. Roosevelt suffered the embolism in his sleep and died without awakening.

Presidential Term: September 14, 1901–March 3, 1909

Age at Inauguration: 42 years, 322 days

Vice President: Charles Warren Fairbanks

Married: Alice Hathaway Lee on October 27, 1880; Edith Kermit Carow on December 2, 1886

Children: Alice Lee Roosevelt, Theodore Roosevelt Jr., Kermit Roosevelt, Ethel Carow Roosevelt, Archibald Bulloch Roosevelt, Quentin Roosevelt

Religion: Dutch Reformed

Education: Harvard College, graduated 1880

Occupation: Author, lawyer, public official

When **THEODORE ROOSEVELT** was a young boy, he bought a dead seal from a fish market and had it stuffed.

Roosevelt owned and could walk on stilts.

Roosevelt is the only U.S. president to have a condom named after him: the Rough Rider.

Before heading off to Harvard in 1876, Roosevelt's father gave him advice regarding the three things on which he should focus his attention and in what order. "Take care of your morals first, then your health, and finally your studies." (One wonders if this is the order of priorities college students would say they follow today.)

Roosevelt once gave a speech after being shot. When the bullet was fired, it struck the folded, fifty-page copy of the speech he had in his jacket pocket. The bullet still entered Roosevelt's body, but the papers had slowed it enough so that it didn't kill him and the damage it did wasn't severe enough to stop him from talking. He probably winged it when he came to the hole (located in the bottom third of the sheet) on each of the fifty pages. "I shall deliver this speech or die," he said. "It is one thing or the other." Upon arriving at the podium, Roosevelt showed the audience his bloody shirt and exclaimed, "It takes more than one bullet to kill a bull moose!"

Roosevelt had a tennis court built on the White House grounds in 1902 and would play all the time, sometimes close to a hundred games a day. He picked his opponents carefully and newspapers referred to his regulars as the "Tennis Cabinet."

Roosevelt had a pet badger named Josiah. He received Josiah as a gift when a little girl threw the badger at the president and he decided to keep him.

Roosevelt was known to leave the Oval Office and run around the Washington Monument to burn off stress.

Roosevelt's favorite breakfast was twelve eggs.

Roosevelt coined the word *muckraker,* and the phrases *lunatic fringe* and *my hat is in the ring.*

When Roosevelt traveled, he always carried a bottle of morphine with him. Roosevelt believed in euthanasia and said that if he contracted something away from his doctor and became incapacitated, he would end his own life with the morphine, rather than linger on in pain.

Roosevelt's nicknames included the Bull Moose, the Driving Force, the Dynamo of Power, Four Eyes, the Great White Chief, the Happy Warrior, Haroun-al-Roosevelt, the Hero of San Juan Hill, the Man on Horseback, the Old Lion, Old Rough and Ready, the Roughrider, Telescope Teddy, Theodore the Meddler, TR, the Trust-Buster, the Typical American, and the Wielder of the Big Stick.

Roosevelt's love of sports is what likely spurred him to hold a boxing match at the White House in which he—Mr. President—would fight a professional boxer. It did not go well. The boxer punched Roosevelt in the left eye and detached his retina, leaving the president blind in that eye.

Roosevelt is responsible for the creation of the Teddy bear stuffed toy. This came about because he brought home a bear cub from a hunting trip and it was immediately dubbed to be the "Teddy" bear.

Roosevelt coined the term *bully pulpit* to describe the impact and power of the White House. The term is still in use today.

Roosevelt had a photographic memory. He reportedly could recite verbatim pages from books he had read years earlier.

Roosevelt hated dirty jokes. The moment he heard something that told him the joke was going blue, he would get up and leave the room.

Roosevelt owned a snake named Emily Spinach.

Roosevelt whipped his children and encouraged the children's teachers to do likewise. After receiving a letter from his son Quentin's teacher requesting that Roosevelt whip the boy for dancing and doodling in class, Roosevelt wrote:

> Don't you think it would be well to subject him to stricter discipline—that is, to punish him yourself. . . . Mrs. Roosevelt and I have no scruples against corporal punishment. We will stand behind you entirely in doing whatever you decide is necessary. . . . If you find him defying your authority or committing any serious misdeed, then let me know and I will whip him.

However, he did caution against excessive physical punishment, too:

> [I]t hardly seems wise to me to start in whipping him for everyday offenses which in point of seriousness look as if they could be met by discipline in school and not by extreme measures taken at home.

Roosevelt is responsible for making college football safer. He insisted that the rules be changed to make play safer or he'd have to ban the game. Why the threat from the president? It was probably because more than a hundred students had died playing the game. Roosevelt correctly concluded that any college sport that results in fatalities should probably be toned down and regulated a bit.

Roosevelt was known to carry a gun in the White House. (One cannot help but wonder how Cabinet meetings went when someone disagreed with the president.)

Today, there is a movement by atheists to have "In God We Trust" removed from American currency (and "under God" removed from the Pledge of Allegiance). This is nothing new. Roosevelt fought for this a hundred years ago.

Roosevelt's inaugural address is unique in the annals of presidential inaugurals. In his almost thousand-word speech, he never uses the word *I*.

Roosevelt owned a one-legged rooster when he was president.

Roosevelt was incredibly prolific. He wrote more than thirty books, as well as countless articles, pamphlets, and speeches, not to mention an estimated 150,000 letters. It is thought he wrote more than eighteen million words throughout his life.

Was Roosevelt the father of texting? Roosevelt supported the 1906 creation of the Simplified Spelling Board. He felt that the English language was too confusing and that the way words were spelled could be simplified. Basically, what this meant was that words would be spelled wrong for ostensible clarity. Words ending in "-ed" were changed to end in "t."

Thus *addressed* became "addresst," *missed* became "mist," and so on. Also, "ough" was changed to "o." Thus, for example, *although* became "altho," and *thorough* became "thoro." He even put forth a resolution to Congress that government documents be written using the Simplified Spelling system. As you might imagine, the British mocked the United States mercilessly (and with good cause, truth be told). The Supreme Court refused to use the dumbed-down spelling and issued a statement that their opinions would be written in the old style. Ultimately, the Simplified Spelling Board was dissolved when its chief financial backer, Andrew Carnegie, died without leaving any funding for the board in his will.

Roosevelt allegedly coined the Maxwell House coffee slogan, "It's good to the last drop!" His exclamation was made spontaneously after being offered a second cup of the coffee at Andrew Jackson's home, the Hermitage, in Nashville, Tennessee.

What Woodrow Wilson said about Roosevelt: "He is the most dangerous of the age."

Roosevelt was Martin Van Buren's third cousin, twice removed.

In 1901, to celebrate the publication of Booker T. Washington's autobiography *Up from Slavery,* Roosevelt invited Washington to have dinner with him at the White House. The response from some Southern politicians was . . . well, let's just say they were racist and disgusting.

His hosting of Booker T. Washington for dinner at the White House notwithstanding, Roosevelt initially felt that giving free blacks and freed slaves the right to vote in 1870 was not the best course of action. In a December 14, 1904, letter to Henry Smith Pritchett, Roosevelt wrote, "I have always felt that the passage of the Fifteenth Amendment at the time it was passed was a mistake." The Fifteenth Amendment to the Constitution (ratified February 3, 1870) reads, "The right of citizens of the United States to vote shall not be denied or abridged by the United States or by any State on account of race, color, or previous condition of servitude."

Roosevelt's last words were "Please put out the light."

Roosevelt has been played in movies by Sidney Blackmer, John Alexander, Brian Keith, William Phipps, Tom Berenger, Robin Williams (twice), and Ed Metzger.

CHAPTER TWENTY-SEVEN

WILLIAM HOWARD TAFT

1909–1913 (Republican)

Born: September 15, 1857

Died: March 8, 1930

Cause of Death: Heart failure caused by arteriosclerotic heart disease, high blood pressure, and chronic bladder inflammation. Taft was serving as Chief Justice of the Supreme Court at the time of his death.

Presidential Term: March 4, 1909–March 3, 1913

Age at Inauguration: 51 years, 170 days

Vice President: James S. Sherman

Married: Helen "Nellie" Herron on June 19, 1886

Children: Robert Alphonso Taft, Helen Herron Taft, Charles Phelps Taft

Religion: Unitarian

Education: Yale College, graduated 1878; Cincinnati Law School, graduated 1880

Occupation: Lawyer, public official

WILLIAM HOWARD TAFT was the biggest president of all time. He stood six feet, two inches tall and weighed in at 332 pounds at his peak. He once got stuck in the White House bathtub and subsequently had an extra-large tub built.

One of Taft's favorite self-deprecating jokes was, "I got off a streetcar and gave my seat to three ladies."

Taft was the only man to serve as both president of the United States and Chief Justice of the Supreme Court, and he might very well have liked being Chief Justice more than he did being president. A few weeks after he was elected president, Taft wrote to a friend, "If I were now presiding in the Supreme Court of the United States, I should feel entirely at home." After being named Chief Justice, he is said to have described the Supreme Court as being what he imagined heaven must be like.

Taft's girth once caused him to rip open the seat of his pants when exiting a carriage, thus exposing the presidential buttocks.

Taft was the first president of the forty-eight contiguous states. Arizona became a state on February 14, 1912, during his administration.

Taft is credited—probably erroneously—with the ritual of the seventh inning stretch at baseball games. The story goes that his three-hundred-plus-pound adiposity was getting more and more uncomfortable sitting in a small wooden chair at a baseball game, so during the seventh inning he stood up and stretched. Seeing the president rise, everyone did likewise and thus the tradition was born. Only it is highly unlikely that this is a true story, although Taft is credited—correctly—with being responsible for the president throwing out the first pitch to open baseball season in 1910. Every president since has done it, except for Jimmy Carter.

Taft fell asleep constantly. Did he suffer from narcolepsy? Or was he just so fat that he was constantly exhausted from carrying around all that weight? He reportedly slept soundly through a Pacific typhoon while visiting the Philippines.

If Taft happened to doze off while working at his desk, his wife, Nellie, would awaken him by putting on an Enrico Caruso record.

Taft's nicknames included Big Bill, Big Chief, Old Bill, and Big Lub.

When Taft was in his early forties, he almost died from dengue fever he contracted during a trip to the Philippines. Dengue fever is a deadly virus spread by mosquitoes.

Nellie Taft was the first First Lady to smoke cigarettes.

What Theodore Roosevelt said about Taft: "[He is a] flub-dub with a streak of the second-rate and the common in him."

Taft loved almonds. In fact, he really loved almonds. He'd eat pounds at a single sitting.

Nellie Taft had the Lincoln bed moved to the attic. Why? She said it was a depressing hulk of a thing that was not conducive to a good night's sleep. (Truth be told, it is quite a formidable bed, measuring six feet wide and eight feet long. Its footboard is decorated with grapes, grapevines, and birds. But still . . .)

Taft had an interesting take on giving women the vote. He was against it . . . unless it could be proven to him that women did, in fact, want to be able to vote. In 1909 he said, "I am not in favor of suffrage for women until I can be convinced that all the women desire it; and when they desire it I am in favor of giving it."

Taft has been played in a movie by Raymond Massey.

CHAPTER TWENTY-EIGHT

WOODROW WILSON

1913–1921 (Democrat)

Born: December 28, 1856

Died: February 3, 1924

Cause of Death: Stroke, complicated by acute asthma. It is believed that Wilson's asthma was caused by the influenza he contracted during the devastating 1918 flu epidemic in America.

Presidential Term: March 4, 1913–March 3, 1921

Age at Inauguration: 56 years, 66 days

Vice President: Thomas R. Marshall

Married: Ellen Louise Axson on June 24, 1885; Edith Bolling Galt on December 18, 1915

Children: Margaret Woodrow Wilson, Jessie Woodrow Wilson, Eleanor Randolph Wilson

Religion: Presbyterian

Education: College of New Jersey (now Princeton University), graduated 1879

Occupation: Teacher, public official

WOODROW WILSON insisted that his morning egg be boiled for thirty minutes.

In a letter Wilson wrote to his wife, he asked, "Are you prepared for the storm of lovemaking with which you will be assailed?"

Wilson was dyslexic, but overcame it. Throughout his life he was staggeringly well educated, earned a Ph.D., and was the author of many acclaimed books about American history. He was also president of Princeton. Not bad for someone with a childhood reading disorder, eh?

While president, Wilson had a ram as a pet. His name was Old Ike and he chewed tobacco.

After Wilson had a stroke at the age of sixty-one, his wife, Edith, essentially took over his duties as president. The public was unaware of the seriousness of Wilson's condition throughout this period.

When Wilson was young, he suffered from ceaseless gastrointestinal woes, including constipation, nausea, diarrhea, heartburn, and other stomach ailments. To combat these troubles, he used a stomach pump to pump coal and water into his stomach. This practice, while commonplace at the time, has since been relegated to use only for drug overdoses.

In 1919, Wilson wrote a poem about his appearance:

> For beauty I am not a star,
> There are others more handsome by far,
> But my face, I don't mind it,
> Because I'm behind it,
> It's the people in front whom I jar.

Wilson had very bad teeth and a very strong tenor voice. He sang in the Princeton glee club.

Wilson's nicknames included the Big One of the Peace Conference, the Phrasemaker, the Schoolmaster, and Woody.

Wilson wrote many of his own speeches. When asked how long it took him to write a speech, he said: "If I am to speak for ten minutes, I need a week for preparation; if fifteen minutes, three days; if half an hour, two days; if an hour, I am ready now."

Wilson's 1916 presidential campaign slogans were "He kept us out of war" and "He proved the pen mightier than the sword."

Wilson was the first U.S. president to travel to Europe while in office. (He went by ship, of course.)

During World War I, Wilson's wife, Edith, wrote an open letter to European women in which she basically pleaded with them not to have sex with American soldiers.

Wilson is the only U.S. president to have earned a Ph.D. So how was he addressed? "Mr. President?" Or "Dr. Wilson?" Guess it depended on the circumstances.

What Theodore Roosevelt said about Wilson: "Byzantine logothete . . . [that] infernal skunk in the White House." (*Logothete* is defined by thefreedictionary.com as "an accountant; under Constantine, an officer of the empire; a receiver of revenue; an administrator of a department.")

The U.S. Treasury once issued a $100,000 bill, and Woodrow Wilson was on it.

Sigmund Freud wrote a book in which he psychoanalyzed Wilson. It wasn't published until both Wilson and his wife had died. In the book, Freud claimed that Wilson was severely dysfunctional, needed to be worshiped, and had been emotionally smothered by his mother.

Wilson was the first president to show a movie in the White House. He chose *The Birth of a Nation*, which had white actors in blackface, depicted the Ku Klux Klan as a noble and patriotic force, and portrayed blacks as sexual predators toward white women and as terribly unintelligent.

In 1915, the *Washington Post* wrote an article about Wilson attending a theater performance with his fiancé, Edith Galt. They wrote, "The President spent most of his time entering Mrs. Galt." "Entering" was supposed to be "entertaining."

Wilson must regrettably be remembered as a president who signed into law a full-blown assault on the First Amendment. The 1918 Sedition Act forbade any "disloyal, profane, scurrilous, or abusive language" about the U.S. government, its flag, or its armed forces or that caused others to view the American government or its institutions with contempt. People were prosecuted and convicted using this blatantly unconstitutional legislation. The law was repealed on December 13, 1920.

Wilson's last words were "I am a broken piece of machinery. When the machinery is broken . . . I am ready."

Wilson is buried in Washington National Cathedral and is the only president buried in Washington, D.C. His second wife, Edith Wilson, is interred alongside her husband. (By the way, the National Cathedral took eighty-three years to build, has

110 gargoyles, 215 stained glass windows, and has an eight-foot, eight-inch-diameter, twenty-four-thousand-pound bell in its fifty-three-bell carillon.) During the 2011 East Coast earthquake, three spires of the National Cathedral broke and fell off the structure. The cathedral was temporarily closed due to the damage.

Wilson has been played in movies by Alexander Knox and Bob Gunton.

CHAPTER TWENTY-NINE

WARREN G. HARDING

1921–1923 (Republican)

Born: November 2, 1865

Died: August 2, 1923

Cause of Death: Stroke, caused by high blood pressure and an enlarged heart, and complicated by pneumonia. Harding was on an arduous tour of America dubbed the "Voyage of Understanding" when he suffered the fatal stroke.

Presidential Term: March 4, 1921–August 2, 1923

Age at Inauguration: 55 years, 122 days

Vice President: Calvin Coolidge

Married: Florence Kling DeWolfe on July 8, 1891

Children: Elizabeth Ann Christian (illegitimate child)

Religion: Baptist

Education: Ohio Central College, graduated 1882

Occupation: Editor-publisher

WARREN HARDING's mother and father were both physicians.

Harding's mother's nickname for her son was Winnie. She called him this because she had wanted to name him Winfield but her husband said no.

Harding had a hard time saying no. At least according to his father, who once reportedly told him, "Warren, it's a good thing you wasn't born a gal . . . [b]ecause you'd be in the family way all the time. You can't say no."

Harding spent time in a psychiatric institution in his twenties after a series of nervous breakdowns.

Harding's 1920 presidential campaign slogans were "Return to Normalcy" and "Cox and Cocktails."

In 1922, the Ku Klux Klan inducted Warren Harding into the Klan at a White House ceremony.

Harding reportedly once lost a complete set of White House china in a poker game.

Harding is the only president about whom the legendary poet E. E. Cummings wrote a poem (although it was not very flattering): "The only man, woman or child / who wrote a simple declarative sentence / with seven grammatical errors."

Something a president could never say today, but that Harding did say: "Let the black man vote when he is fit to vote, prohibit the white man voting when he is unfit to vote."

Harding was a horny guy, and he indulged himself regularly. One of his paramours was a woman named Carrie Phillips. Florence Harding was aware of what was going on but wasn't happy about it, of course. When Phillips showed up at one of Harding's front porch political speeches, Florence threw a piano stool at her. Phillips wisely fled.

Harding served alcohol at White House parties during his administration. It apparently didn't matter to him that the Eighteenth Amendment—Prohibition—was still in effect.

Harding's nicknames included the Shadow of Blooming Grove and Wobbly Warren.

Charles Forbes, the guy Harding personally picked to run the Veterans Administration (then the Veterans Bureau), made a lot of money selling off stuff belonging to VA hospitals and pocketing the cash.

Harding's wife, Florence, was the first First Lady to vote.

Harding had an affair with Nan Britton before and when he was president and fathered a child with her. She wrote about once doing the deed with Harding in a White House Oval Office coat closet.

Harding once said of his presidency, "I am not fit for this office and never should have been here."

Harding had very big feet. How big? you ask. He wore a size fourteen shoe, that's how big. (George Washington, Abraham Lincoln, and Bill Clinton are runners-up with size thirteen feet.)

What Woodrow Wilson said about Harding: "He has a bungalow mind."

How many cups of coffee can you get out of a pound of coffee? Around forty-five six-ounce cups or thirty-two eight-ounce cups. Florence Harding insisted that the White House cooks get sixty cups out of a pound of coffee.

When Harding died, the rumor spread that his wife had poisoned him in retaliation for his cheating on her. The truth was never known because his wife refused permission to perform an autopsy before Harding was buried. The official story was that he died of a stroke.

Harding was portrayed by Malachy Cleary in HBO's series *Boardwalk Empire*.

CHAPTER THIRTY

CALVIN COOLIDGE

1923–1929 (Republican)

Born: July 4, 1872

Died: January 5, 1933

Cause of Death: Coronary thrombosis (heart failure caused by a blood clot in the heart). For months before his death, Coolidge had complained of the classic symptoms of heart disease, such as breathlessness, fatigue, weakness, and abdominal symptoms which were attributed to indigestion, but which were more than likely angina pains.

Presidential Term: August 3, 1923–March 3, 1929

Age at Inauguration: 51 years, 29 days

Vice President: Charles G. Dawes

Married: Grace Anna Goodhue on October 4, 1905

Children: John Coolidge, Calvin Coolidge Jr.

Religion: Congregationalist

Education: Amherst College, graduated 1895

Occupation: Lawyer

One of **CALVIN COOLIDGE**'s pre-presidential jobs was toy maker.

Coolidge's favorite breakfast was boiled raw wheat and rye and he liked to have his head rubbed with Vaseline while he ate it. (Yes, you read that right.)

Coolidge had two pet lions as president.

Coolidge also had a pet pygmy hippopotamus. His name was Billy.

Coolidge slept at least ten hours a day: eight to ten hours each night, plus a two- to four-hour nap every afternoon.

Coolidge once shook hands with nineteen hundred people in thirty-four minutes at a White House reception.

Coolidge owned a raccoon. He would put a leash on it and walk the White House grounds.

Thanks to Coolidge, American Indians are now Native Americans, in the literal sense. During his administration, Coolidge signed legislation making Indians American citizens.

Coolidge's nicknames included Silent Cal, Cautious Cal, Cool Cal, and the Sphinx of the Potomac.

Coolidge's 1924 presidential campaign slogan was "Keep Cool and Keep Coolidge."

Coolidge liked baggy underwear. (Could Coolidge have served as an object lesson for *Seinfeld*'s Kramer, who once remarked, "I need the secure packaging of Jockeys. My boys need a house"?)

Today, we take lots of things for granted. Like antibiotics. Yet in Coolidge's day, antibiotics were a good twenty years away from being developed and available. In 1924, Coolidge's son Calvin Jr. developed a blister on his foot playing tennis. It got infected, turned into blood poisoning, and the boy died shortly thereafter. He was only sixteen years old.

Coolidge is the one who came up with the phrase, "The business of America is business."

Coolidge was a big fan of the old-fashioned custom of sitting on one's front porch after dinner. In pre-air-conditioning days, this was a way of relaxing after eating and catching whatever cooling breezes would come your way as the sun set. After Coolidge entered the White House in 1923, he decided he wanted to continue this custom. He did so enjoy it, and he initially didn't factor in how this particular leisure pursuit might be a little different now that he was president of the United States. So out he went onto the front porch which, of course, was the White House North Portico, with its towering columns, marble stairs, and Tiffany glass windows. Unfortunately, this hoped-for moment of relaxation did not go as planned. When the president of the United States is sitting in a chair at the entrance to the White House, people will stop and stare. And they did. The crowds that formed on Pennsylvania Avenue quickly dissuaded Coolidge from takin' it to the streets after dining.

Coolidge and his family members were very cautious about being unwittingly overheard. When they were concerned about the wrong ears hearing what they were saying, they communicated in sign language.

Coolidge was the only U.S. president born on the Fourth of July.

Is this story about Coolidge true? Well, if it isn't, it oughta be. Coolidge and the First Lady visited a farm one day where Grace was told that a rooster would have sex several times a day. "Tell that to Mr. Coolidge," the First Lady said, probably with a smirk. So the farmer did exactly that, to which the president responded, "With the same hen?" The farmer shook his head no. Coolidge (likewise smirking, we hope) said, "Tell that to Mrs. Coolidge."

Coolidge went to work as a daily newspaper columnist following his presidency. He received a dollar a word and one cannot help but wonder if this inspired him to be somewhat more verbose than he might have been if he were being paid a flat rate. It was in one of Coolidge's daily columns that he penned his definition of unemployment: "When more and more people are thrown out of work, unemployment results."

On the day he died, Coolidge worked on a jigsaw puzzle of George Washington.

Writer Dorothy Parker, when told of Coolidge's death, responded, "How could they tell?" His nickname Silent Cal was obviously right on the money.

One of Coolidge's well known traits was being a man of few words. He was, shall we say, legendarily taciturn. Thus the classic story about Coolidge that took place at a party: He was approached by the hostess, who said, "You must talk to me, Mr. President. I made a bet today that I could get more than two words out of you." Coolidge replied, "You lose."

Coolidge has been played in a movie by Ian Wolfe.

CHAPTER THIRTY-ONE

HERBERT HOOVER

1929–1933 (Republican)

Born: August 10, 1874

Died: October 20, 1964

Cause of Death: Massive internal bleeding caused by gastrointestinal hemorrhages secondary to intestinal cancer. Hoover was ninety years old when he died and the first time he ever underwent a surgical procedure—an operation to remove a diseased gallbladder—was when he was eighty-four years old. Strong stock, eh?

Presidential Term: March 4, 1929–March 3, 1933

Age at Inauguration: 54 years, 206 days

Vice President: Charles Curtis

Married: Lou Henry on February 10, 1899

Children: Herbert Clark Hoover, Allan Henry Hoover

Religion: Society of Friends (Quaker)

Education: Stanford University, graduated 1895

Occupation: Engineer

When he was a kid, **HERBERT HOOVER** picked bugs off potatoes. He earned $1 for every hundred bugs. So not only did he have to pick them off, he had to save them and count them.

During World War I, Hoover, as head of the U.S. Food Administration, cut food supplies in America by 15 percent to guarantee food for soldiers overseas. This tactic was called "Hooverizing."

Before becoming president, Hoover used his degree in geology to identify bountiful gold mines around the globe as a freelance mining consultant. He bought stakes in many of these gold mines and was a multimillionaire by the time he was forty. He once remarked that if a man "has not made a million dollars by the time he is forty he is not worth much." Ironically as president he was unable to put an end to the Great Depression.

Hoover's 1928 presidential campaign slogans were "A chicken in every pot. A car in every garage." "Hoo but Hoover?" and "We are turning the corner."

Hoover did not like to set his eyes on the White House servants—ever. Whenever he or the First Lady appeared anywhere where a servant was present, he or she had to run into a closet and remain there until the coast was clear. Groundskeepers had to hide behind bushes. These people lived with the fear of being fired if Hoover caught a glimpse of one of them.

Hoover donated his presidential salary to charity. He was the first and only president to do so.

Hoover's nicknames included the Chief, the Great Engineer, and the Great Humanitarian.

Hoover insisted on wearing a suit and tie when fishing. (There are pictures.)

Hoover never delivered his State of the Union addresses in person. He sent Congress written copies only.

Hoover and his wife, Lou, spoke in Mandarin Chinese when they were discussing private matters and did not want to be overheard talking.

Hoover took a lot of grief for his failure to pull the country out of the Great Depression. A "Hoover Hotel" was a cardboard shack. A "Hooverville" was a shantytown of cardboard shacks.

Lou Hoover once got a nasty letter from a pissed-off White House visitor. What horrific incident had so roused this citizen's ire? She had seen a curtain during her White House tour that had obviously been mended. (The horror!)

Hoover is the president who decided that "The Star-Spangled Banner" would be the National Anthem of the United States.

When Hoover went Christmas shopping one year, reporters and photographers followed him and printed in the paper every gift he bought. No surprises that year on Christmas morning in the Hoover White House, eh?

Hoover refused to dance, because of his "faith and ignorance," he said.

Ever hear of Herberta or Hooveria? They're, respectively, an asteroid and a small planet that were each named for Herbert Hoover. The main-belt asteroid 1363 Herberta was discovered on August 30, 1935, and the minor planet 932 Hooveria, which orbits the Sun, was discovered on March 23, 1920.

What Calvin Coolidge said about Hoover: "That man has offered me unsolicited advice for six years, all of it bad."

Sound familiar? Hoover once said, "Blessed are the young for they shall inherit the national debt."

Hoover believed America had generational problems that were the cause of all the ongoing governmental problems. He phrased this concern in one of his most memorable quotes: "If we could have one generation of properly born, trained, educated and healthy children, a thousand problems of government would vanish."

Hoover was once officially denounced by the Texas state legislature. Why? He had invited the black wife of a congressman to tea at the White House.

Hoover has been played in a movie by Thomas Peacocke.

CHAPTER THIRTY-TWO

FRANKLIN D. ROOSEVELT

1933–1945 (Democrat)

Born: January 30, 1882

Died: April 12, 1945

Cause of Death: Cerebral hemorrhage caused by high blood pressure and arteriosclerosis. Roosevelt's arteries were so clogged his morticians had a great deal of trouble embalming his body. The embalming fluid would not flow through his heavily blocked arteries.

Presidential Term: March 4, 1933–April 12, 1945

Age at Inauguration: 51 years, 33 days

Vice Presidents: John N. Garner, Henry A. Wallace, Harry S Truman

Married: Anna Eleanor Roosevelt on March 17, 1905

Children: Anna Eleanor Roosevelt, James Roosevelt, Elliott Roosevelt, Franklin Delano Roosevelt Jr., John Aspinwall Roosevelt

Religion: Episcopalian

Education: Harvard College, graduated 1903; Columbia Law School, attended

Occupation: Public official, lawyer

Genealogists have confirmed with certainty that **FRANKLIN DELANO ROOSEVELT** was related to an astonishing eleven presidents: Washington, the two Adamses, Madison, Van Buren, the two Harrisons, Taylor, Grant, Theodore Roosevelt, and Taft. And he was also related to Winston Churchill. He was a fourth cousin, once removed of Ulysses S. Grant; a fourth cousin, three times removed of Zachary Taylor; and a fifth cousin of Theodore Roosevelt.

FDR was nameless for seven weeks after his birth.

FDR attended the Groton School for Boys when he was, well, a boy. (The school still exists and is now called just the Groton School.) His headmaster there was Endicott Peabody. Peabody went on to study for the ministry and officiated at FDR's marriage to Eleanor. Of Peabody, FDR said, "As long as I live his influence will mean more to me than that of any other people next to my father and mother." Peabody had influence elsewhere, too: in Tombstone, Arizona. He moved out there for a period in 1882 and helped build St. Paul's Episcopal Church—using some of Wyatt Earp's gambling winnings. (Also, Peabody's great-granddaughter is actress Kyra Sedgwick, wife of actor Kevin Bacon.)

FDR was a C student at Harvard.

FDR dropped out of Columbia Law School in 1905 because he didn't need the law education. He successfully passed the New York bar exam without it.

FDR never used hand gestures when he spoke in front of a group because he had to hold on to the podium with both hands to prevent falling down. He had contracted polio as a child and, because of the resultant paralysis, used heavy metal leg braces so he could stand in one place when speaking. The American public never knew.

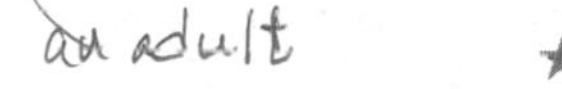

FDR on public speaking: "Be sincere; be brief; be seated."

FDR's 1932 presidential campaign slogan was "I propose (to the American people) a New Deal." His 1936 campaign slogan was "Remember Hoover!" (Ouch.) His 1944 campaign slogan was "We are going to win this war and the peace that follows."

What Herbert Hoover said about FDR: "[FDR was a] chameleon on plaid."

According to Eleanor Roosevelt, her husband was so busy as president that on occasion their sons had to make appointments to see him.

FDR may have been the only U.S. president to have been photographed knitting, although it was probably a joke. Shortly after Eleanor and Franklin were married they posed for a photograph on the steps of FDR's family estate in Hyde Park, New York. Eleanor was holding a cocktail glass and Franklin was knitting. Their expressions were totally serious (always the best indicator of a prank), and it is believed they were, in a sense, playfully "swapping" each other's main interests.

When FDR was recovering from polio, he wrote a screenplay telling the story of Old Ironsides. It wasn't picked up.

★

What a difference a word makes. The original draft of FDR's Pearl Harbor speech had "a day that will live in world history." FDR crossed out "world history" and wrote in "infamy."

FDR was afraid of the number thirteen. This is called triskaidekaphobia. He would invite his secretary to have dinner with him if the table would seat thirteen people without her. And he wouldn't leave for a trip on the thirteenth of the month under any circumstances.

Frank Sinatra claimed that he named his son Frank Sinatra Jr. not after himself, but after FDR. Frank Jr.'s full name is Franklin Wayne Emmanuel Sinatra.

FDR's 1940 presidential campaign slogan was "Better a Third Term Than a Third-Rater."

FDR's nicknames included the Boss, Deficit, FDR, the Featherduster of Dutchess County, the Gallant Leader, Houdini in the White House, the Kangaroosevelt, the Man in the White House, Mr. Big, the New Dealer, the Raw Dealocrat, Roosocrat, the Sphinx, the Squire of Hyde Park, and A Traitor to His Class.

There are 125,000 photos of Franklin Delano Roosevelt in the FDR Presidential Library. Exactly two show him in a wheelchair. Yes, the press was much more accommodating of presidents' wishes in those days.

Speaking of wheelchairs, when the FDR Memorial in Hyde Park, New York, was opened, it depicted a statue of Roosevelt, seated, with a cloak over his lower body. At the very rear of the statue, two small wheels could be seen, but there was no real acknowledgment that he was in a wheelchair. Advocates for the disabled were less than thrilled about this and claimed that the statue downplayed the tremendous achievements even someone with a disability could achieve. Ultimately, they won. A new statue of FDR was unveiled in July 1998 showing him seated in the wheelchair he personally designed and in which he spent twenty years of his life. FDR's grandson David was initially opposed to showing his grandfather in a wheelchair but changed his mind and came to believe that the statue would inspire people and convince them that no matter what their physical limitations, they, too, could achieve great things in their life.

Eleanor Roosevelt was a member of the Daughters of the American Revolution. When she learned that the DAR was refusing to allow black singer Marian Anderson to perform in a DAR hall, she immediately resigned, and then had Anderson sing on the steps of the Lincoln Memorial.

FDR's favorite movie was *I'm No Angel,* starring Mae West.

FDR is the only president to have been elected to four terms (although he served only three; he died on the eighty-third day of his fourth term). He won in 1932, 1936, 1940, and 1944. Afterward legislation was passed limiting presidents to two terms. (Although many people believe wholeheartedly that it should be repealed.)

FDR had a stamp collection consisting of twenty-five thousand stamps in forty albums. He specialized in stamps from the Western Hemisphere and Hong Kong. It sold for more than $200,000 after his death.

FDR wrote a second Bill of Rights. What would America be like today if all these rights had been enacted legislatively? FDR recorded a speech in which he spelled out his second Bill of Rights:

In our day certain economic truths have become accepted as self-evident. A second Bill of Rights under which a new basis of security and prosperity can be established for all—regardless of station, or race, or creed.

Among these are:

The right to a useful and remunerative job;

The right to earn enough to provide adequate food and clothing and recreation;

The right of every farmer to raise and sell his products at a return which will give him and his family a decent living;

The right of every businessman, large and small, to trade in an atmosphere of freedom; freedom from unfair competition and domination by monopolies at home or abroad;

The right of every family to a decent home;

The right to adequate medical care and the opportunity to achieve and enjoy good health;

The right to adequate protection from the economic fears of old age, sickness, accident, and unemployment;

The right to a good education.

All of these rights spell security. And after this war is won we must be prepared to move forward, in the implementation of these rights, to new goals of human happiness and well-being.

For unless there is security here at home there cannot be lasting peace in the world.

FDR's last words before he died were "I have a terrific headache." The headache was actually a cerebral hemorrhage. He died shortly thereafter.

FDR has been played in movies by Jack Young, Ralph Bellamy, Edward Herrmann (three times), Dan O'Herlihy, Jason Robards, Jon Voight, and Kenneth Branagh.

CHAPTER THIRTY-THREE

HARRY S TRUMAN

1945–1953 (Democrat)

Born: May 8, 1884

Died: December 26, 1972

Cause of Death: Systemic failure caused by heart failure complicated by lung congestion and kidney malfunction. (Truman was one of the few presidents to die in a hospital.)

Presidential Term: April 12, 1945–January 20, 1953

Age at Inauguration: 60 years, 339 days

Vice President: Alben W. Barkley

Married: Elizabeth "Bess" Virginia Wallace, June 28, 1919

Children: Mary Margaret Truman

Religion: Baptist

Education: University of Kansas City Law School, attended

Occupation: Farmer, public official

There is no period after the "S" in **HARRY S TRUMAN**. That's how it was written on his birth certificate.

Truman had diphtheria when he was eight years old. He was treated with the standard remedy of the time: a half tumbler of whiskey. The idea was that the sufferer would "retch up" the disease.

One of Truman's pre-presidential jobs was bank clerk.

Truman drank two ounces of bourbon every day, usually before meals.

Truman practiced the piano every morning for two hours beginning at 5:00 before getting on with his presidential duties.

Some of Truman's ancestors were Confederates.

Truman was once named one of the Ten Best Dressed Senators on Capitol Hill.

Truman got his famous "The Buck Stops Here" slogan from prison. During a visit to the El Reno Federal Reformatory in Oklahoma, Truman saw the sign over the warden's desk and immediately adopted its message as his own. An identical sign was made by the prisoners for President Truman and sent to him on October 2, 1945. It is now on display at the Truman Library, where it has been since 1957.

Another of Truman's famous sayings was, "If you can't stand the heat, get out of the kitchen." He loved the saying and said it a lot, and some historians think he may have originated it.

When Truman was a senator, the saying that he had displayed on his desk was from Mark Twain: "Always do right. This will gratify some people and astonish the rest."

When Truman was vice president, he attended a National Press Club gathering and decided to play the piano for the crowd. As he was playing, someone convinced then-twenty-year-old actress Lauren Bacall to sit on top of the piano. She did so, and flashed a whole bunch of leg while up there. Bess Truman later opined that it was time for Harry to give up the piano.

Truman was responsible for the design of the Seal of the President of the United States used today. When he became president, he noticed that the eagle's head on the seal was turned toward the arrows. He ordered the seal redesigned so that the eagle's head always faced the olive branch.

Truman called psychiatrists "nut doctors."

Truman's nicknames included Give 'Em Hell Harry, Mister Missouri, the Senator from Pendergast, the Haberdasher, and High Tax Harry.

Sound familiar? At a speech in Akron, Ohio, on October 11, 1948, Truman said, "The Republicans favor a minimum wage—the smaller the minimum the better."

Truman's 1947 State of the Union address was the first broadcast on television.

Truman's 1948 presidential campaign slogans were "I'm just wild about Harry" and "Pour it on 'em, Harry!"

After his presidency, Harry and Bess Truman moved in with her mother. His mother-in-law, who believed—and stated frequently—that Harry had never amounted to anything, also lived in the White House when he was president.

Truman once noted that the presidents he felt made the "greatest contribution to the maintenance of the republic" were Washington, Jefferson, Jackson, Polk, Lincoln, Cleveland, Wilson, and both Roosevelts.

Truman once described the U.S. Constitution as "a plan, but not a straitjacket." He also noted, "Read it one hundred times, and you'll always find something new."

Truman was a supporter of the superiority of women, once noting, "I've always thought that the best man in the world is hardly good enough for any woman."

Truman installed a dental office in the White House.

Truman got into the army during World War I by memorizing the eye chart. He was terribly nearsighted so he knew that was the only way to pass the test.

In 1946, shortly after Truman took office, a leg of the piano his daughter, Margaret, played broke through the ceiling of what is now the Private Dining Room. The ceiling was repaired as part of the extensive renovation to the White House during the Truman years.

Truman was dismissive of Sigmund Freud, psychiatry, and psychiatrists, especially when they got involved in the educational system, once remarking that, "Kids should learn more fundamental reading, writing, and arithmetic. Freud psychology and nut doctors should be eliminated."

Truman was the great-great-great nephew of President John Tyler.

Truman's favorite prayer was the Prayer to Do What's Right. It read:

> O Almighty and Everlasting God, Creator of Heaven, Earth, and the Universe, help me to be, to think, to act what is right, because it is right. Make me truthful, honest, and honorable in all things; make me intellectually honest for the sake of right and honor and without thought of reward to me. Give me the ability to be charitable, forgiving, and patient with my fellow men. Help me to understand their motives and their shortcomings, even as thou understandest mine! Amen.

Truman was totally against term limits. In his book, *Mr. Citizen,* he called the Twenty-Second Amendment "one of the worst ever added to the Constitution. It is as bad as that short-lived Prohibition Amendment." His philosophy regarding term limits was simple: "It is the historic background of our ideals and institutions that will prevent dictatorship, not the Twenty-Second Amendment."

Truman's favorite books were Marquis James's books on Andrew Jackson, Claude Bowers's books on Jefferson, and a collection of Jefferson's letters called *A Jefferson Profile*. He also liked Carl Sandburg's books about Lincoln, Thomas Benton's memoirs, and Ulysses S. Grant's autobiography. He loved the George Washington Papers, which were published by the U.S.

government. He also read the Bible many times, Plutarch, and *The Rise and Fall of the Roman Empire.*

Truman disliked Picasso and other modern painters. "They are lousy," he once said. "Any kid can take an egg and a piece of ham and make more understandable pictures."

Truman once had his pilot buzz the White House in the presidential plane, the *Sacred Cow,* while his wife and daughter were on the roof. He forgot to tell the Secret Service of his plans, and of course, they immediately thought the White House was under attack.

Truman's criteria for the presidency boiled down to two things: someone honorable and someone who has a great deal of experience in government.

Truman believed that freedom and liberty were worth more than peace.

Truman supported vegetarianism in concept, believing that "we have no more moral right to murder a horse, cow, or hog than we have one another." But he did eat meat nonetheless.

Truman was a lousy speller and believed that spelling was created by Satan.

Truman believed in the great importance of reading, once remarking, "Readers of good books, particularly books of biography and history, are preparing themselves for leadership. Not all readers become leaders. But all leaders must be readers."

Truman was a stated fan of the architecture and beauty of a number of famous buildings, including the Parthenon, the Taj Mahal, St. Paul's Cathedral in London, York Minster, Chartres Cathedral, the Dome of the Rock in Jerusalem, the capitol buildings of several states (Mississippi, West Virginia, Utah, and Missouri), the New York Life Building, the Sun Insurance building in Montreal, the Parliament Building in London, La Madeleine in Paris, the Palace of Versailles, and Basilica of St. Mark and the Doge's Palace in Venice.

Can you imagine this happening today? When the *Washington Post* published Paul Hume's negative review of Margaret Truman's singing (Hume noted that she "cannot sing very well, is flat a good deal of the time . . . has not improved in the years we have heard her"), Truman personally wrote the following letter and mailed it himself:

THE WHITE HOUSE
Washington
Dec. 6, 1950

Mr. Hume:

I've just read your lousy review of Margaret's concert. I've come to the conclusion that you are an "eight ulcer man on four ulcer pay."

It seems to me that you are a frustrated old man who wishes he could have been successful. When you write such poppy-cock as was in the back section of the paper you work for it shows conclusively that you're off the beam and at least four of your ulcers are at work.

Some day I hope to meet you. When that happens you'll need a new nose, a lot of beefsteak for black eyes, and perhaps a supporter below!

Pegler, a gutter snipe, is a gentleman alongside you. I hope you'll accept that statement as a worse insult than a reflection on your ancestry.

H.S.T.

(The "Pegler" Truman referred to was Westbrook Pegler, a popular columnist of the time.) In 1951, Hume sold the original letter for $3,500. It ended up in the Malcolm Forbes estate, and is now owned by the Harlan Crow Library in Highland Park, Texas. President Clinton had a copy of the letter hanging in his office.

One night as Truman lay sleeping in the White House, the skies exploded with a violent rainstorm accompanied by close-to-hurricane-speed winds. Truman jumped out of bed and ran around checking the White House windows to see if any rain was getting in. It was. In buckets. So what did the president do? Did he summon armies of servants and Secret Service agents to take care of the flooding? No. He grabbed as many towels as he could from the White House bathrooms and ran around trying to mop up the water. Only after White House ushers saw what was happening did he receive assistance. His daughter, Margaret, wrote of the incident, "It had simply never occurred to Dad to call out to anyone for help, any more than he would have sought assistance had the same thing happened in our home in Missouri."

Truman and his daughter corresponded ceaselessly. Truman would often include a few dollars for Margaret as well as interesting clippings or memorabilia he thought she'd like. In a letter in June 1946, Truman included a bill to tune the White House piano from Andrew Jackson's administration. The cost? $1.50.

Bess Truman did not like the laundry facilities at the White House, or in all of Washington, D.C., for that matter. She solved this problem by mailing her and Harry's dirty laundry back to Independence, Missouri, to be washed. Imagine receiving bundles of dirty clothes in the mail . . . wouldn't want to be the mailman tasked with that job.

Truman has been played in movies by James Whitmore, E. G. Marshall, Ed Flanders, Gary Sinise, and David Patrick Kelly.

CHAPTER THIRTY-FOUR

DWIGHT D. EISENHOWER

1953–1961 (Republican)

Born: October 14, 1890

Died: March 28, 1969

Cause of Death: Congestive heart failure. Eisenhower suffered a heart attack while president and many more during his retirement, his heart growing less efficient with each subsequent attack. Eisenhower's heart could not handle the pneumonia he developed following a minor operation in early 1969, and this is what ultimately killed him.

Presidential Term: January 20, 1953–January 20, 1961

Age at Inauguration: 62 years, 98 days

Vice President: Richard M. Nixon

Married: Mary "Mamie" Geneva Doud on July 1, 1916

Children: Doud Dwight Eisenhower, John Sheldon Doud Eisenhower

Religion: Presbyterian

Education: U.S. Military Academy at West Point, graduated 1915

Occupation: Soldier (general)

DWIGHT D. EISENHOWER was a great cook. His best dishes were cornmeal pancakes, vegetable soup, and charcoal-broiled steaks.

Eisenhower (and his siblings) were raised as Jehovah's Witnesses. He later was baptized as a Presbyterian.

Eisenhower was, at least once, an exhibitionist. During his time at West Point, when ordered to report to a corporal and to be wearing his dress coat, he showed up wearing *only* his dress coat. He was naked from the waist down.

Eisenhower was greatly enamored (cough) of his staff driver Kay Summersby. Ike's nickname for her? Private Parts.

Eisenhower couldn't stand Communist-hunter Senator Joseph McCarthy and refused to engage him in discussing "Commies" in the U.S. government. He once memorably described such an unlikely event as a "pissing contest."

Many presidents played golf. However, for all the chief executives' time on the links, Eisenhower is the only U.S. president to hit a hole in one. He was seventy-seven when he hit it in 1968.

Eisenhower's 1952 presidential campaign slogan was "I Like Ike." His 1956 slogans were "I Still Like Ike" and "Peace and Prosperity."

Eisenhower's nicknames included Ike, Swede, and the Kansas Cyclone.

Eisenhower made close to half a million dollars on royalties for his book about World War II, *Crusade in Europe,* which was published in 1948. He wrote the book himself without the help of ghostwriters. The book was a huge success and outsold everything but Dr. Spock's classic child-care book and the Bible.

On October 7, 1957, Ghana finance minister Komla Agbeli Gbedemah was kicked out of a Dover, Delaware, diner because they refused to serve "colored people." Three days later, Eisenhower remedied the ignorant, racist insult by having Gbedemah at the White House for breakfast.

Eisenhower was the only president to serve in the military in both World War I and World War II.

Every Valentine's Day, Ike wore what he and Mamie called his "love bug" boxer shorts. They were embroidered with red hearts.

Between 1955 and 1957, Eisenhower had some major health problems while serving as president. In 1955, he had a heart attack. In 1956, he had intestinal bypass surgery. In 1957, he had a stroke. But he recovered from everything and served two terms, until his leaving office in 1961.

When Harry S Truman was president, Grover Cleveland's widow, Frances Cleveland (then Frances Preston) visited the White House for lunch. She was introduced to Eisenhower, who had just led the Allies to victory in Europe. Ike did not recognize her or know who she was. Trying to be polite, he asked her, "And where did you live in Washington, ma'am?" Her response can only lead us to ask if generals blushed. "In the White House," she replied.

Only eleven presidents out of forty-four, beginning with Eisenhower, have been president of all fifty states. Hawaii became the fiftieth state on August 21, 1959, during Eisenhower's term.

Eisenhower always carried three lucky coins in his pocket: a silver dollar, a five-guinea gold piece, and a French franc.

Eisenhower did not have a favorite color. (Mamie's were pink, yellow, and green.)

What Harry Truman said about Eisenhower: "The General doesn't know any more about politics than a pig knows about Sunday."

Ike's favorite dessert was prune whip.

Eisenhower's favorite movie was *The Big Country*, starring Gregory Peck.

Eisenhower started painting when he was fifty-eight years old and had a small studio in the White House. He preferred to paint scenic landscapes, and some of his paintings today sell for in excess of $1,000.

Ike had a somewhat mangled off-the-cuff speaking style that he became quite famous for. In 1957, political journalist Doris Fleeson hilariously rewrote Lincoln's Gettsyburg Address in "Ikespeak":

> I haven't checked these figures, but eighty-seven years ago, I think it was, a number of individuals organized a governmental setup here in this country. I believe it covered certain Eastern areas, with this idea they were following up based on a sort of national independence arrangement and the program that every individual is just as good as every other individual.

When asked, Eisenhower said his favorite books were the complete works of Shakespeare, the Bible, and *A Connecticut*

Yankee in King Arthur's Court. He also said he liked reading Westerns for relaxation.

Eisenhower was the first president to travel by jet and helicopter.

Eisenhower's last words were "I want to go; God take me."

Eisenhower has been played in movies by Henry Grace, Robert Beer, Keene Curtis, and Tom Selleck.

CHAPTER THIRTY-FIVE

JOHN F. KENNEDY

1961–1963 (Democrat)

Born: May 29, 1917

Died: November 22, 1963

Cause of Death: Assassinated. Kennedy was shot through the throat and in the head while riding in a motorcade in Dallas, Texas. He never regained consciousness and died from his wounds shortly after the shooting.

Presidential Term: January 20, 1961–November 22, 1963

Age at Inauguration: 43 years, 236 days

Vice President: Lyndon B. Johnson

Married: Jacqueline "Jackie" Lee Bouvier on September 12, 1953

Children: Caroline Bouvier Kennedy, John Fitzgerald Kennedy Jr., Patrick Bouvier Kennedy

Religion: Roman Catholic

Education: Harvard College, graduated 1940

Occupation: Author, public official

The teenaged **JOHN F. KENNEDY**'s Choate nickname was Rat Face.

★

In 1951, Jacqueline Bouvier interviewed Congressman John F. Kennedy for the *Washington Times Herald*. She married him two years later.

★

During the 1960 presidential election, J. Edgar Hoover released candid photos of JFK frolicking naked on a beach with a gorgeous brunette.

★

Actor Peter Lawford admitted taking pictures of JFK and Marilyn Monroe sharing a bath together, as Marilyn performed oral sex on the president.

JFK's right leg was three quarters of an inch longer than his left. He wore shoes that corrected the disparity.

JFK's 1960 presidential campaign slogan was "A time for greatness."

JFK was essentially on speed while president. His personal physician, Max "Dr. Feelgood" Jacobson, routinely injected him with a drug cocktail consisting of amphetamines, steroids, vitamins, and, according to some sources, monkey placenta. (Jacobson's other patients included Yul Brynner, Truman Capote, Cecil B. DeMille, Marlene Dietrich, Mickey Mantle, Zero Mostel, Anthony Quinn, Nelson Rockefeller, and Tennessee Williams.) He took one of these cocktails just before the famous 1960 Kennedy–Nixon debate, which established Kennedy as a viable presidential contender and endeared him instantly to millions of Americans.

JFK took testosterone pills daily during his presidency. (This explains a lot, don't you think?)

It was said (and apparently witnessed) that JFK could read four newspapers cover to cover in twenty minutes.

JFK's IQ, according to a school entrance exam, was 119.

Jackie Kennedy's favorite movie was Federico Fellini's *La Dolce Vita*.

Kennedy's nicknames included Jack, JFK, and the King of Camelot.

JFK was so popular in Massachusetts that a guy who worked at a razor factory named John F. Kennedy got himself elected state treasurer just by getting his name on the ballot.

During something known as the PT-109 incident, JFK swam four hours (with a bad back) towing an injured seaman by his life jacket strap. An impressive detail: Kennedy towed the guy with his teeth.

In 1951, at the age of thirty-four, JFK contracted a fever while visiting Japan. His temperature hit 106 degrees, which is almost always fatal for humans, but he survived.

Reportedly, JFK would frequently leave movies at the halfway mark. Apparently, many films bored him.

JFK may have been a sex addict. Or maybe the drugs he was on just made him constantly horny. According to Democratic Party operative Bobby Baker, Kennedy once said to him, "I get a migraine headache if I don't get a strange piece of ass every day." Yet, there are other sources that quote JFK as saying, "If I don't have a woman every three days or so I get a terrible headache." Regardless of whether it was a daily requirement or an every-three-days requirement, I think we can be sure that JFK got a headache if he didn't get laid.

In addition to his Addison's disease, back problems, colitis, steroid complications, and other recurring ailments, JFK also suffered from the STD chlamydia.

The first Sunday after his inauguration, JFK was being driven across Washington when he asked the driver to cruise by his old residence on N Street in Georgetown. When they arrived at the house, Kennedy was horrified to see piles of newspapers on the front steps. "Look at all those newspapers piled up all over the front step. I told them and *told* them to cancel deliveries out here. Probably some of my Republican neighbors are already spreading the story. 'How can he run the country when he can't organize his own home?' " So what did the new president do? He jumped out of the limousine (much to the horror of the Secret Service), ran to the steps, picked up all the old newspapers, and threw them into the backseat of the car.

Presidents like to be held in high regard by the public and the press. However, JFK probably got a big kick out of what his young daughter, Caroline, told the White House press corps one day. When a reporter asked what her father was doing, she responded, "Oh, he's upstairs with his shoes and socks off not doing anything."

Jackie Kennedy is the only First Lady of whom naked photos have been published. In 1975, Larry Flynt published in his *Hustler* magazine paparazzi photos of Jackie sunbathing nude on Skorpios Island in 1971.

According to a book about Jackie published on the fiftieth anniversary of JFK's first year in office, JFK bluntly mocked the idea of Lyndon Johnson becoming president. According to interviews with Jackie, JFK and his brother Robert even plotted ways to prevent him getting the Democratic nomination in future elections. Jackie is quoted as saying, "Jack said it to me sometimes. He said, 'Oh, God, can you ever imagine what would happen to the country if Lyndon were president?' . . . And Bobby told me that he'd had some discussions with him . . . do something to name someone else in 1968."

It was Lee Harvey Oswald's third shot that killed JFK. (Oswald fired three shots, hitting Kennedy with two.) If Secret Service agents had been allowed to stand on the presidential limousine's running boards, standard operating procedure would have been for an agent to throw himself on top of the president after the first or second shot. Kennedy refused to allow agents to ride on the running boards, thus there was no one to protect him from the kill shot. The common wisdom today is that Kennedy probably would have lived if an agent had been in place and acted as trained. It was also Kennedy's decision to not have the bulletproof dome on the car that afternoon. He said he wanted to be closer to the people.

The first doctor to attend to JFK after he was shot had delivered Lee Harvey Oswald's daughter Audrey a month earlier.

JFK has been played in movies by Cliff Robertson, James Franciscus, William Petersen, Bruce Greenwood, Brett Stimely, and John Allen Nelson.

CHAPTER THIRTY-SIX

LYNDON B. JOHNSON

1963–1969 (Democrat)

Born: August 27, 1908

Died: January 22, 1973

Cause of Death: Cardiac arrest caused by arteriosclerosis. The heart attack that killed LBJ woke him from a nap. He managed to call one of his Secret Service agents but he died on the way to the hospital.

Presidential Term: November 22, 1963–January 20, 1969

Age at Inauguration: 55 years, 87 days

Vice President: Hubert H. Humphrey

Married: Claudia "Lady Bird" Alta Taylor on November 17, 1934

Children: Lynda Bird Johnson, Luci Baines Johnson

Religion: Disciples of Christ

Education: Southwest Texas State Teachers College (now Texas State University–San Marcos), graduated 1930; Georgetown University Law Center (attended 1934)

Occupation: Teacher, public official

LYNDON B. JOHNSON was unnamed for the first three months of his life. Everyone just called him "Baby."

Lyndon B. Johnson worked as a shoe-shine boy and a trash collector when he was young.

LBJ was the only U.S. president to be sworn in on an airplane. His first presidential order was "Let's get airborne."

LBJ loved to give people electric toothbrushes.

Secretary of Defense Robert McNamara, during a visit to the White House with his wife, brought LBJ some fresh cheese blintzes. The Secret Service destroyed them because presidents are not allowed to eat "outside" food for safety reasons. LBJ was livid when he heard what they had done. "What in the hell happened to my cheese blintzes?" he hollered. "You leave my food alone!"

LBJ was a huge fan of Fresca, a grapefruit-flavored soda. He loved it so much he had a special button installed in the Oval Office specifically used to summon a Fresca from the galley.

LBJ's 1964 presidential campaign slogan was "All the way with LBJ."

Retired Secret Service agent Richard Roth is quoted in *In the President's Secret Service* as saying, "If Johnson weren't President, he'd be in an insane asylum."

LBJ was very well endowed and was not averse to proudly proving it now and then, often by displaying his penis to unsuspecting female journalists.

An Air Force One steward reported that LBJ would frequently be completely naked in front of his daughters and female secretaries.

"Son, they're all my helicopters." This was LBJ's response to an aide who had pointed out to him which helicopter was his, as in "That's your helicopter, Mr. President."

LBJ's weight varied by ten or fifteen pounds a month.

LBJ was a nasty drunk, and he was often drunk when he was president. If he didn't like something a Secret Service agent said or if agents refused to follow his orders for safety reasons, he was not averse to whacking the agents in the head with a newspaper—and then firing them.

Lady Bird Johnson once walked in on Johnson having sex with one of his secretaries on a couch in the Oval Office.

LBJ once memorably described the presidency in the following way: "Being President is like being a jackass in a hailstorm. There's nothing to do but stand there and take it."

LBJ's Oval Office desk chair was a remodeled helicopter seat. It was green and had a built-in ashtray.

Johnson's nicknames included Big Daddy, Landslide Lyndon, Light-Bulb Lyndon, Bullshit Johnson, and LBJ.

LBJ once ordered six pairs of pants and specifically requested the clothes maker ensure there was plenty of room in the crotch.

LBJ would urinate on the lawn of his ranch in front of reporters. While urinating outside one day, LBJ accidentally splashed a Secret Service agent's legs with presidential urine.

He shrugged it off and reminded the agent that being pissed on by the president was the president's prerogative.

LBJ once held a press conference with White House pool reporters while sitting on the toilet moving his bowels.

When he was president, LBJ insisted on breakfast in bed every day. And he got it.

For all his womanizing ways, LBJ was responsible for some of the most far-reaching and beneficial social programs and legislative advancements in American history, including the Civil Rights Act, the Voting Rights Act, the establishment of Medicare and Medicaid, and the creation of HUD, the Department of Housing and Urban Development.

LBJ once received a 1915 fire truck as a gift.

LBJ owned a German-made Amphicar. It was a lagoon blue convertible and it could travel on land and water. LBJ enjoyed taking friends for a ride in the car, feigning brake failure, and driving into a lake. As his passengers panicked and tried to escape what they believed was certain death from drowning, LBJ would laugh hysterically. (Wasn't he a sketch?)

LBJ has been played in movies by Donald Moffat, Randy Quaid, Tom Howard, and Michael Gambon.

CHAPTER THIRTY-SEVEN

RICHARD NIXON

1969–1974 (Republican)

Born: January 9, 1913

Died: April 22, 1994

Cause of Death: Stroke.

Presidential Term: January 20, 1969–August 9, 1974

Age at Inauguration: 56 years, 11 days

Vice Presidents: Spiro T. Agnew, Gerald R. Ford

Married: Thelma "Patricia" Catherine Ryan on June 21, 1940

Children: Patricia "Tricia" Nixon, Julie Nixon

Religion: Society of Friends (Quaker)

Education: Whittier College, graduated 1934; Duke University Law School, graduated 1937

Occupation: Lawyer, public official

The Watergate break-in is not the only break-in to which **RICHARD NIXON** was connected. When he was a student at Duke Law School, he and two accomplices broke into a dean's office to check their grades before they were posted.

Nixon was related to two other U.S. presidents. He was William Howard Taft's seventh cousin, twice removed. He was Herbert Hoover's eighth cousin, once removed.

Nixon's high school nickname was "Nicky." He absolutely hated it.

One of teenaged Nixon's jobs was as a barker at the Wheel of Fortune booth at the Slippery Gulch carnival in Prescott, Arizona.

Nixon's favorite foods were spaghetti, cottage cheese, and meat loaf.

Nixon had motion sickness and hay fever his entire life. One cannot help but wonder how he dealt with the multitude of vehicles and traveling he had to do as president.

Nixon originally wanted to be an FBI agent. He was rejected by the bureau.

Nixon's 1968 presidential campaign slogan was "This time, vote like your whole world depended on it."

A Secret Service agent once saw Nixon taste one of his dog's dog biscuits.

Richard Nixon wore a suit and dress shoes when he walked on the beach.

Richard Nixon meditated, although he probably would not have described his practice as such. He greatly enjoyed long periods of silence during which he would simply sit still and not speak. This almost certainly would qualify as a form of meditation.

Pat Nixon was the first First Lady to earn a graduate degree. (It was in education.)

Nixon's mouth was once washed out with soap. Figuratively. The Richard M. Nixon Fountain on the north lawn of Nixon's alma mater Whittier College was deliberately loaded with soap detergent so that the fountain would spew suds, as a prank. It cost $400 to repair the pump.

Nixon's nicknames included Gloomy Gus, the Iron Butt, the Mad Monk, the New Nixon, and Tricky Dick.

In 1963, Nixon appeared as a guest on *The Jack Paar Show*. He played an original song on the piano.

According to the *Guinness Book of World Records*, Nixon holds the record for appearing on the most covers—fifty-five—of *Time* magazine.

Nixon's favorite movie was *Patton*, starring George C. Scott.

First Lady Pat Nixon was once photographed smoking in a restaurant. When asked about it, the White House press secretary said that she "didn't inhale." (Sounds familiar.)

Nixon pardoned Jimmy Hoffa, the labor union leader who had been convicted of bribery and fraud and had served time in prison. In 1975, Hoffa disappeared and was declared legally dead in 1982.

When Elvis Presley visited Nixon at the White House, he presented him with a handgun as a gift, a gun he had simply walked into the White House carrying. Yikes. Good thing Elvis was a fan of Nixon, telling him in a letter, "I was nominated this coming year one of America's Ten Most Outstanding Young Men. . . . I believe that you, Sir, were one of the Top Ten Outstanding Men of America also."

Nixon was so paranoid he once ordered the Secret Service to tap his brother Donald's phone.

Being a First Daughter has its perks. When her father was president, Tricia Nixon hosted a party at the White House with the popular band the Turtles ("Happy Together," "Elenore") providing the music.

Nixon had new uniforms designed for the White House police. These outfits had gold trim, big hats, and other pompous adornments and were mocked mercilessly. They ended up being donated to a high school marching band, which tells us all we need to know about what these uniforms looked like.

Nixon is responsible for having the words *shit* and *fuck* published in the pages of the *New York Times.* During the Watergate scandal, it was discovered that some of the secret tape recordings Nixon had made in the Oval Office included him uttering those four-letter words, and others. The *New York Times* actually printed verbatim transcripts of the tapes, with the obscene words included. At the time, *Times* executive editor A. M. Rosenthal was quoted as saying, "We take 'shit' from the President but from nobody else." "Expletive deleted" soon became the accepted euphemism for the president's (and other's) more colorful vocabulary on the Watergate tapes.

Nixon, the only U.S. president to resign the office of the presidency, left very specific instructions regarding the disposition of his personal papers. In his will he wrote:

> I direct my executors to collect and destroy my "personal diaries." [T]he property constituting my "personal diaries" shall be subject to the following restrictions: At no time shall my executors be allowed to make public, publish, sell, or make available to any individual other than my executor . . . the contents or any part or all of my "personal diaries" and, provided further, that my executors shall . . . destroy all of my "personal diaries." My "personal diaries" shall be defined as any notes, tapes, transcribed notes, folders, binders, or books that are owned by me or to which I may be entitled under a judgment of law including, but not limited to, folders, binders, or books labeled as Richard Nixon's Diaries, Diary Notes, or labeled just by dates, that may contain my daily, weekly or monthly activities, thoughts or plans. The determination of my executors as to what property is included in this bequest shall be conclusive and binding upon all parties interested in my estate; however, it is my wish that my executors consult with my surviving daughters and/or my office staff in making this determination.

Nixon said (on his Oval Office tapes) the following about Italians: "They're not like us. They smell different, they look different, they act different. The trouble is, you can't find one that's honest." (One of the reasons your humble author and sixth-generation Italian-American was not a fan of Richard Nixon.)

Unbelievably, Nixon was the first president to visit all fifty American states. Not a single president before Nixon had taken the time to travel to every state.

A student protester once gave Nixon the finger. The president gave one back to him.

Nixon claimed to have never had a headache his entire life.

What John F. Kennedy said about Nixon: "Do you realize the responsibility I carry? I'm the only person standing between Nixon and the White House."

Nixon made some interesting statements through the years, including the following.

- "If you think the United States has stood still, who built the largest shopping center in the world?"
- "I won't shake hands with anybody from San Francisco."
- "I would have made a good Pope."
- "I was under medication when I made the decision to burn the tapes."

Nixon has been played in movies by Philip Baker Hall, Anthony Hopkins, Dan Hedaya, Frank Langella, and Robert Wisden.

CHAPTER THIRTY-EIGHT

GERALD FORD

1974–1977 (Republican)

Born: July 14, 1913

Died: December 26, 2006

Cause of Death: Arteriosclerotic cerebrovascular disease and diffuse arteriosclerosis. Ford died on the thirty-fourth anniversary of Harry S Truman's death.

Presidential Term: August 9, 1974–January 20, 1977

Age at Inauguration: 61 years, 26 days

Vice President: Nelson A. Rockefeller

Married: Elizabeth "Betty" Bloomer Warren, October 15, 1948

Children: Michael Gerald Ford, John Gardner Ford, Steven Meigs Ford, Susan Elizabeth Ford

Religion: Episcopalian

Education: University of Michigan, graduated 1935; Yale University Law School, graduated 1941

Occupation: Lawyer, public official

GERALD FORD's real first name was Leslie.

Ford was a male model when he was young.

Ford was given offers to play professional football for the Green Bay Packers and Detroit Lions.

Ford campaigned for Congress on his wedding day.

Ford is the only man to ever serve as both vice president and president, yet not have been elected to either office.

During his presidency, Ford ate the exact same thing for lunch every day: a scoop of cottage cheese covered with A-1 steak sauce, a sliced onion or quartered tomato, and a small scoop of butter pecan ice cream. (Is it me, or does this concoction sound not the least bit appealing?)

Ford was a public "wind breaker." And whenever he did toot his own horn, so to speak, he would always put the blame on a Secret Service agent standing nearby.

Ford's nicknames included Jerry and Mr. Nice Guy.

Ford was known to the Secret Service as a (cough) "frugal" man. His usual tip to a bellman or a caddy was a buck.

Ford once wrote a definition of a successful marriage, which included, "There must be a belief on the part of both that there is nothing of a higher priority than the sanctity and continuation of the relationship."

When comedian Chevy Chase was in rehab in the Betty Ford Clinic in the mid-1980s, he and his wife were invited to have lunch with Ford and his wife, Betty. The plan was for them to watch screen tests of actors who had tried out for the role of Gerald Ford in an upcoming TV movie about Betty Ford (*The Betty Ford Story*, 1987; Josef Summer eventually got the role). When Jayni Chase and Betty Ford couldn't figure out how to hook up the VCR, Chevy stood up to help. Ford sat him down again and said, "No, no, Chevy. Don't even think about it. I'll probably get electrocuted, and you'll be picked up and arrested for murder."

Ford was the first U.S. president to visit Japan.

Because he was never elected president, Ford did not give an inaugural address upon his swearing in as president. He did, however, deliver "Remarks on Taking the Oath of Office as President."

Lyndon Johnson once said of Ford, "He's a nice fellow but he spent too much time playing football without a helmet."

Ford's favorite TV shows were *Movin' On* and *Kojak*.

Ford's most famous pardon was, of course, of Richard Nixon. What most people don't know is that he also pardoned Civil War Confederate general Robert E. Lee and restored his U.S. citizenship 110 years after the pardon was requested. Lee's original request was found in the National Archives and Ford decided to grant the request.

President and Mrs. Ford slept in the same room and in the same bed in the White House. (They were, after all, married.) This had not been done since the administration of Calvin Coolidge; presidents and First Ladies had their own separate bedrooms. Betty Ford consistently received hate mail chastising her for her "inappropriate" sleeping arrangements. Betty ignored the criticism, except for a sharp remark in which she said that apparently to some people, a president is supposed to be a eunuch.

Ford has been played in movies by Dick Crockett, Larry Lindsay, Corbin Bernsen, and Neal Matarazzo.

CHAPTER THIRTY-NINE

JIMMY CARTER

1977–1981 (Democrat)

Born: October 1, 1924

Presidential Term: January 20, 1977–January 20, 1981

Age at Inauguration: 52 years, 111 days

Vice President: Walter F. Mondale

Married: Eleanor Rosalynn Smith on July 7, 1946

Children: John William "Jack" Carter, James Earl "Chip" Carter III, Donnel Jeffrey "Jeff" Carter, Amy Lynn Carter

Religion: Baptist

Education: Georgia Southwestern College, 1941–1942; Georgia Institute of Technology, 1942–1943; United States

Naval Academy, 1943–1946 (class of 1947); Union College, 1952–1953

Occupation: Farmer, public official

JIMMY CARTER was the first president born in a hospital. Every president born before 1924 had been born at home.

Carter's "real" name is James Earl Carter Jr. However, everyone knew him as Jimmy and called him Jimmy. And no highfalutin' event like a presidential inauguration was going to change that for our good ole Southern boy president. Carter was the first—and only—president to be sworn in with his nickname. "I, Jimmy Carter, . . ."

Carter once insulted all of Mexico by admitting that he had gotten diarrhea during a stay in Mexico City. He added to the insult by referring to his problem as "Montezuma's revenge," which is perceived by Mexicans as a Yankee slur.

Shortly after moving into the White House, Rosalynn Carter picked up a phone and asked to be connected to Jimmy. "Jimmy who?" was the White House operator's response.

Carter was intent on portraying the image of a common, down-to-earth man. He'd carry his own suit bag so the photographers could snap a pic of him, little knowing the bag was empty and just for show.

Carter is the only president who has published a novel. It was *The Hornet's Nest* and was published in 2003. It is about the Revolutionary War. Its opening line is "The young girl stood quiet and unseen behind the trunk of a large walnut tree, its leaves and branches scarred on one side by a recent fire."

Did Carter once leave his nuclear launch code card—the "biscuit"—in a suit that was sent to the dry cleaners? No one who would know will confirm or deny the story.

Carter refused to allow the aide carrying the nuclear briefcase "football" to stay on his property when he went home to Georgia. The aide ended up a ten-mile drive away from Carter. (Think the bombs would have landed by the time the football got to Plains?)

Carter is related to Elvis.

Carter's favorite movie is *Gone With the Wind*.

Carter wears one soft contact lens.

Carter has and frequently wears a lucky red tie.

Carter's nicknames included Jimmy and President Malaise.

Carter can read 2,000 words a minute. The average is around 120 words per minute.

Carter's favorite hymns are "Amazing Grace," "Blest Be the Tie That Binds," and "The Navy Hymn."

Carter once caused a media uproar when he did something that some people apparently believed was a political ploy to boost his popularity: He changed the direction of the part of his hair. (Yeah, that oughta do it.)

In 1979, Carter was attacked by a rabbit while fishing alone in a rowboat in Plains, Georgia. Well, he wasn't actually attacked, although the relentlessly mocking press coverage of the incident certainly suggested that he was. The truth is that a swamp rabbit swam out to Carter's boat and apparently wanted to climb aboard. Carter shooed it away by splashing water on it with an oar. In Carter press secretary Jody Powell's 1986 autobiography *The Other Side of the Story*, he wrote of the incident:

> The animal was clearly in distress, or perhaps berserk. The President confessed to having had limited experience with enraged rabbits. He was unable to reach a definite conclusion about its state of mind. What was obvious, however, was that this large, wet animal, making strange hissing noises and gnashing its teeth, was intent upon climbing into the Presidential boat.

Later, folk singer Tom Paxton wrote a song about the incident called "I Don't Want a Bunny Wunny."

Carter's favorite book is *Let Us Now Praise Famous Men* by James Agee. He also considers *War and Peace* one of his favorite books.

Carter is the only U.S. president who has admitted seeing a UFO. He told the *National Enquirer* in 1976:

> I am convinced that UFOs exist because I've seen one. . . . It was a very peculiar aberration, but about 20 people saw it. . . . It was the darndest thing I've ever seen. It was big; it was very bright; it changed colors; and it was about the size of the moon. We watched it for 10 minutes, but none of us could figure out what it was.

He went on to say, "If I become President, I'll make every piece of information this country has about UFO sightings available to the public and the scientists," and "One thing is for sure. I'll never make fun of people who say they've seen unidentified objects in the sky!" His observation took place one evening in October 1969 at 7:15 in Leary, Georgia. With him were ten members of the Leary, Georgia, Lions Club, who corroborated his account.

As president, Carter continued to teach a Bible study class and chastised the members of his staff who were single and living together for "living in sin."

During an overnight stay at the Carter White House after a performance, Willie Nelson smoked a joint on the White House roof.

Rosalynn Carter is the only First Lady to be photographed with a serial killer. During a campaign stop, she was photographed with John Wayne Gacy, a serial killer who ultimately raped and murdered thirty-three young boys. He was a Democratic organizer at the time the picture was taken.

When Carter's daughter, Amy, got married, she chose not to have her father give her away. Her reason? She said she "belonged to no one." She also kept her own last name.

What Gerald Ford said about Carter: "Teddy Roosevelt . . . once said 'Speak softly and carry a big stick.' Jimmy Carter wants to speak loudly and carry a fly swatter."

Carter was an eclectic pardoner. During his administration he pardoned Peter Yarrow of Peter, Paul, and Mary; Patty Hearst; Confederate President Jefferson Davis; and all the Vietnam draft dodgers.

Carter hosted the International Jazz Festival at the White House in 1978. At the legendary Dizzy Gillespie's request, Carter went up onstage and sang the song "Salt Peanuts" with the band. This probably did not tax the president's vocal abilities, or require him to memorize lyrics. The song's lyrics consist of singing "Salt peanuts, salt peanuts" between elaborate jazzy musical breaks.

What might be Carter's most famous quote came during a *Playboy* interview in 1976: "I've looked on many women with lust. I've committed adultery in my heart many times. God knows I will do this and forgives me."

Carter has been played in movies by Ed Beheler (twice).

CHAPTER FORTY

RONALD REAGAN

1981–1989 (Republican)

Born: February 6, 1911

Died: June 5, 2004

Cause of Death: Alzheimer's disease.

Presidential Term: January 20, 1981–January 20, 1989

Age at Inauguration: 69 years, 349 days

Vice President: George H. W. Bush

Married: Jane Wyman on January 26, 1940 (divorced, 1948); Nancy Davis on March 4, 1952

Children: Maureen Elizabeth Reagan, Michael Edward Reagan, Patricia Ann Reagan, Ronald Prescott Reagan

Religion: Disciples of Christ

Education: Eureka College, graduated 1932

Occupation: Actor, public official

When **RONALD REAGAN** was a teenager, he worked as a lifeguard at Lowell Park on the Rock River in Illinois and rescued seventy-seven people from drowning, none of whom ever tipped him. He did, however, once receive a $10 tip for rescuing a swimmer's dentures from the bottom of the river.

One of Reagan's pre-presidential jobs was circus roustabout.

Reagan was considered for the role of Mr. Braddock in *The Graduate.*

Reagan was rejected for the movie *The Best Man*. The role he got turned down for was the president of the United States. They said he didn't look like a president.

A 1942 Warner Brothers press release stated, "Ann Sheridan and Ronald Reagan co-star for the third time in Warner's *Casablanca.*" Was Reagan actually up for the role that was ultimately played by Humphrey Bogart? No. This press release was for publicity only and to keep Warner's top players' names in the news. Apparently, press releases weren't required to be factual.

At age sixty-nine, Reagan was the oldest elected president.

At Reagan's inaugural balls, guests ate forty million jelly beans.

Secret Service agents routinely sweep hotel rooms the president will be staying in for electronic bugs. Sometimes they find bugs intended for the previous guest. Once, when sweeping a room before Reagan's visit, the Secret Service did, indeed, find a bug that had been placed to eavesdrop on the guest who had recently checked out. The guest? Elton John.

Reagan admitted to being claustrophobic.

Reagan's nicknames included the Defender, Dutch, the Gipper, the Great Communicator, the Oldest and the Wisest, and the Teflon President.

Reagan's 1984 presidential campaign slogans were "Are You Better Off Than You Were Four Years Ago?" and "Morning Again in America."

During Reagan's term in office, a man showed up at the White House gate carrying a live chicken and demanding to see the president. Why? He wanted to perform a blood sacrifice for him using the chicken. When he was denied entrance, the man slammed the chicken onto one of the sharp spear-like posts of the fence surrounding the grounds, killing it and, apparently, succeeding in performing his ritual sacrifice for Reagan. The guy ended up in a mental institution.

According to journalist Lou Cannon, Reagan was greatly influenced by the pacifist speech delivered by the alien in the movie *The Day the Earth Stood Still.*

When Reagan was president, Air Force One was often told when to take off and land by Nancy Reagan's astrologer.

Reagan's two favorite movies were *Dirty Harry,* starring Clint Eastwood, and *Rambo,* starring Sylvester Stallone.

Reagan once rhetorically asked, "What does an actor know about politics?"

Reagan's favorite TV show was *Family Ties.*

Reagan never was nominated for or won an Academy Award. However, a short film he narrated called *Beyond the Line of Duty* did win a 1942 Oscar for Best Short Film.

In 1985 Reagan needed a biopsy on a piece of suspicious tissue taken from his nose. To prevent news leaks, the tissue was sent for biopsy under the name of Ms. Tracy Malone, supposedly a sixty-two-year-old white female. The tissue turned out to be a basal cell carcinoma, a malignancy more than likely caused by excessive lifetime sun exposure. The White House subsequently issued a statement that "a small area of irritated skin"

had been "submitted for routine studies for infection and it was determined no further treatment is necessary."

When Reagan was prescribed a hearing aid it took the press two weeks to notice, according to his doctor, and once they did, hearing aid sales went up 75 percent.

Reagan had a rather self-deprecating take on his presidency, once saying, "The thought of being President frightens me and I do not think I want the job." Some other choice quotes include the following:

- "It's true hard work never killed anybody, but I figure, why take the chance?"
- "I have left orders to be awakened at any time in case of national emergency—even if I'm in a Cabinet meeting."
- "I never drink coffee at lunch. I find it keeps me awake for the afternoon."

Reagan has been played in movies by Rip Torn, Jay Koch (three times), Bryan Clark, Richard Crenna, and Fred Ward.

CHAPTER FORTY-ONE

GEORGE H. W. BUSH

1989–1993 (Republican)

Born: June 12, 1924

Presidential Term: January 20, 1989–January 20, 1993

Age at Inauguration: 64 years, 222 days

Vice President: J. Danforth Quayle

Married: Barbara Pierce on January 6, 1945

Children: George Walker Bush, Robin Bush, John Ellis "Jeb" Bush, Neil Bush, Marvin Bush, Dorothy "Dora" Bush

Religion: Episcopalian

Education: Yale University, graduated 1948

Occupation: Businessman, public official

GEORGE H. W. BUSH's great-great grandfather, James Bush, was one of the forty-niners who headed to California during the late 1800s Gold Rush. James died on his way back east.

When Bush moved his family to Odessa, Texas, in 1948, his apartment neighbors were prostitutes, specifically a mother-daughter team with whom the Bushes had to share a bathroom.

When Bush was serving in the navy during World War II, he heard that one of the gruesome practices the Japanese employed on captured prisoners was ritualistic cannibalism. (Usually they ate the liver of their vanquished enemy.) Bush, who weighed only 160 pounds at the time, commented, "I'd have been like an hors d'oeuvre for the poor guy."

Bush was the "lucky" Republican who was given the assignment to officially request the resignation of Richard Nixon on behalf of the GOP.

When Bush, then vice president, returned to Washington after the shooting of Ronald Reagan in 1981, his aides urged him to take a helicopter to the White House after landing in D.C. Bush refused, saying, "Only the President lands on the South Lawn." Bush's helicopter landed near the vice presidential residence, and he then drove to the White House.

In Japan these days, if you puke, you are said to have *Bushu-suru*: "done the Bush thing." This new word was coined after Bush vomited at a banquet hosted by the prime minister of Japan in 1992.

Bush is related to four other U.S. presidents (besides his son). He is Franklin Pierce's fifth cousin, four times removed. He is Theodore Roosevelt's seventh cousin, three times removed. He is Abraham Lincoln's seventh cousin, four times removed. He is Gerald Ford's eleventh cousin, once removed.

Bush's favorite movie is *Chariots of Fire*.

Bush's nicknames included Poppy, 41, Bush the Elder, and Papa Bush.

Bush was the youngest navy pilot in U.S. history.

Bush hated broccoli. He loathed the redolent weed and actually went so far as to ban it from any and all White House dinners and events.

Bush and his wife, Barbara, both suffer from the rare Graves's disease, an autoimmune disorder. The odds of a husband and wife both contracting Graves's are estimated at one in three million. The Bushes' dog Millie had lupus, which is also an autoimmune disease. Doctors estimate that the odds of two people and a dog all contracting an autoimmune disease are one in twenty million. Because of these odds, in 1991, the Secret Service had the water tested at the White House, Camp David, and the Bush family home in Maine.

Bush appeared on *Saturday Night Live* after Dana Carvey's impression of him became widespread and very popular. Bush's lines were, "It's totally exaggerated! It's not me. Those crazy hand gestures. The pointing thing. I don't do 'em!"

Bush could mangle syntax and grammar with the best of them. Here are a few personal favorites, all guaranteed to have been uttered by our forty-first president:

- Boy, they were big on crematoriums, weren't they? (1989, at Auschwitz)
- Let me give you a little serious political advice. One single word. Puppies. Worth the points. (1990)
- When I need a little advice about Saddam Hussein, I turn to country music. (1991)
- You cannot be president of the United States if you don't have faith. Remember Lincoln, going to his knees in times of trial and the Civil War and all that stuff. You can't be. And we are blessed. So don't feel sorry for—don't cry for me, Argentina. Message: I care. (1992)
- Ozone Man, Ozone. He's crazy, way out, far out, man. (1992, about Al Gore)
- It gets into quota, go into numerical, set numbers for doctors or for, it could go into all kinds of things.
- For seven and a half years I've worked alongside President Reagan. We've had triumphs. Made some mistakes. We've had some sex . . . uh . . . setbacks.
- I have opinions of my own, strong opinions, but I don't always agree with them.

- American freedom is the example to which the world expires.

Bush claims to have coined the phrase "You da man" in the early 1960s. According to his daughter, Dora, Bush was moved to shout it to the Houston Astros' Rusty Staub as he ran home. He says it caught on from there.

Bush has been played in movies by John Roarke, Daniel T. Healy, and James Cromwell.

CHAPTER FORTY-TWO

BILL CLINTON

1993–2001 (Democrat)

Born: August 19, 1946

Presidential Term: January 20, 1993–January 20, 2001

Age at Inauguration: 46 years, 154 days

Vice President: Albert Gore Jr.

Married: Hillary Rodham on October 11, 1975

Children: Chelsea Victoria Clinton

Religion: Baptist

Education: Georgetown University, graduated, 1968; Ox-

ford University, attended 1968–1970; Yale University Law School, graduated 1973

Occupation: Lawyer, public official

BILL CLINTON was the first presidential Rhodes Scholar.

Clinton will always be remembered as the U.S. president most adept at world-class parsing. During his grand jury testimony concerning the Monica Lewinsky scandal, Clinton is on record as responding to a question with, "It depends on what the meaning of the word 'is' is."

Christopher Anderson, writing in *Bill and Hillary: The Marriage*, reported a rumor that Clinton had felt up a woman in a bathroom . . . during his own wedding reception.

Comedian Bill Maher once called Clinton "a hard dog to keep on the porch."

Clinton once told the audience during an MTV appearance that he wears jockey shorts.

When Clinton tore a tendon in his knee in 1997 and needed surgery, the operation was performed at the National Naval Medical Center in Bethesda, Maryland. Dozens of surgeons participated in the relatively routine surgical procedure, so each one could say they operated on the president of the

United States. Each surgeon would do a tiny little thing: an incision, exposing the tendon, and so forth. According to the Secret Service agents assigned to oversee the security of the operating room, the operation took hours.

Clinton's nicknames include Bill, Bubba, Slick Willie, the Comeback Kid, the First Black President, Boy Governor, and the MTV President.

It's likely that Clinton will go down in U.S. history as the tardiest president of all time. He was almost always late for things, and it didn't matter the circumstances. He reportedly left a Supreme Court justice and the king of Spain cooling their heels while he did whatever he did. (You can write your own joke here if you like.)

Clinton had a unique, folksy, casual speaking style. In 1992, he once described the American citizen's right to privacy as "to give people a good lettin' alone."

In 1995, Clinton was playing golf at a golf club in Wyoming. Nearby were houses under construction. A Secret Service agent surveying the surrounding area spotted a man on the roof of one of the houses being built. The man had a rifle pointed at Clinton and was looking through the rifle's scope. Of course, he was quickly apprehended and brought in for questioning. Was the man an assassin? Was he hoping to pick off the president from that roof? No. He was simply using the rifle's telescopic scope to get a better look at Clinton. It apparently never occurred to him that someone pointing a rifle at the president might get the Secret Service's attention.

In 1996, upon seeing a newly discovered Inca mummy, Clinton said, "You know, if I were a single man, I might ask that mummy out. That's a good-looking mummy!"

Clinton is lactose intolerant.

Clinton played saxophone in a jazz trio when he was in high school. They were called Three Blind Mice, and their trademark was wearing sunglasses onstage.

Clinton once lost the "biscuit"—the card the president carries that provides him with the code numbers required to launch a nuclear attack. He is supposed to have it with him at all times. The numbers on the card will allow the president access to the "football"—the black briefcase that would be used to issue the nuclear launch orders.

Clinton's favorite TV show is *Grey's Anatomy*.

Clinton's 1992 presidential campaign slogans were "For people, for a change," "It's the economy, stupid," "It's time to change America," and "Putting people first."

Clinton once owned a 1970 El Camino pickup. He installed AstroTurf in the back and never explained why.

Clinton's mother had no eyebrows. She drew them in.

Clinton is the only president who, as president, shook hands with Cuban politician Fidel Castro.

Clinton's two favorite movies are *High Noon* and *Casablanca*.

Clinton was the first white person to be inducted into the Arkansas Black Hall of Fame.

Clinton collects miniature saxophones.

Clinton pardoned his brother Roger Clinton Jr. after Roger served a year in prison for cocaine possession.

As a young girl, Hillary Clinton wanted to be an astronaut. When she wrote to NASA about how to go about applying for the job, they responded that space was for men only.

Some of Clinton's most interesting statements through the years have included the following:

- I'm someone who had a deep emotional attachment to Starsky and Hutch.
- I may not have been the greatest president, but I've had the most fun eight years. (Hmm.)

- When I was in England, I experimented with marijuana a time or two, and I didn't like it. I didn't inhale and never tried it again.
- Look, half the time when I see the evening news, I wouldn't be for me, either.

Clinton has been played in movies by Craig Barnett, Timothy Watters, and Scott Herriott.

CHAPTER FORTY-THREE

GEORGE W. BUSH

2001–2009 (Republican)

Born: July 6, 1946

Presidential Term: January 20, 2001–January 20, 2009

Age at Inauguration: 54 years, 198 days

Vice President: Richard B. Cheney

Married: Laura Welch on November 5, 1977

Children: Barbara Pierce Bush, Jenna Welch Bush

Religion: Methodist

Education: Yale University, graduated 1968; Harvard Business School, graduated 1975

Occupation: Businessman

In 1976, at the age of thirty, **GEORGE W. BUSH** was arrested for driving under the influence (DUI). He was fined $150 and lost his license.

Bush knows a good line when he hears one. In remarks following the attack on the World Trade Center, Bush said, "This despicable act of terror will not stand." Ten years earlier, his father, President George H. W. Bush, said of Iraq's invasion of Kuwait that it "will not stand."

Bush holds the record for having the highest *and* the lowest approval ratings of any president in U.S. history.

Bush has a picture of himself posing with ZZ Top. It is said to be one of his favorite photos.

Bush supported capital punishment and private ownership of handguns. His Methodist religion did not. His ultimate position? Paraphrased, he basically said, the whole country is not Methodist and I'm not going to make decisions based on the beliefs of those who are.

In high school, Bush was a head cheerleader.

Bush's nicknames have included George W., Dubya, Bushtail, the Bombastic Bushkin, Lip, Tweeds Bush, and Temporary. The last one was when he joined the Skull and Bones Society at Yale and couldn't come up with a secret name he liked.

Bush once called a reporter a "major league asshole."

Bush's favorite TV show is A&E's *Biography*.

Bush runs at 7.5 miles an hour. His Secret Service agents have to ride bicycles to keep up with him.

Bush graduated from Yale with a low C average. Typically, a "low C" means a C–, which is a 70–72 cumulative grade point average.

Laura Bush is the only First Lady to give birth to twins.

There exists a George W. Bush Talking Action Figure. It has a computer chip in it that allows it to speak twenty-five phrases—in George W's actual voice. It comes with a certificate of authenticity.

When Bush was drinking, he once challenged his father to a fight. The elder Bush didn't take him up on his challenge and instead expressed disappointment in his son.

Once, when his father was president, George W. Bush was put under Secret Service protection because of intelligence that said the entire Bush family had been targeted for assassination. The younger Bush drove himself around, but the Secret Service car was right behind him. And because they were right behind him, they crashed into the back of his car when the future president, apparently uncertain as to whether to try to make it through a yellow light or stop, ultimately decided to stop short.

Bush does not allow anyone to speak negatively of his father in his presence.

Librarian Laura Bush was devoted to her chosen career. By the time she and George met, the books in her bedroom were categorized according to the Dewey decimal system.

Bush is reportedly a very competitive person. His friends have said that when he was young, they all had to keep playing until George won.

Bush's route to a speech was changed at the last minute by the Secret Service because Patsy Henigman, a psychic with an impressive track record, had reported a vision in which she saw the president shot by a sniper on an overpass. She saw Bush in a casual jacket and an open shirt, and she saw him sitting behind the driver instead of rear right, which is where he was supposed to sit. When agents saw Bush dressed as Henigman had described and watched him get into the presidential limo and sit behind the driver, they changed the route immediately to avoid the overpass that was, indeed, on the originally designated route. (Better to be safe than sorry, right?)

Bush was eating a soufflé in a restaurant when President Obama called him to tell him Osama bin Laden had been killed.

★

Just like his father, Bush could mangle a statement with the best (worst?) of them. Here is a sampling of some of the more memorable remarks that actually gushed forth from the mouth of our forty-third president:

- I didn't grow up in the ocean—as a matter of fact—near the ocean—I grew up in the desert. Therefore, it was a pleasant contrast to see the ocean. And I particularly like it when I'm fishing. (2008)
- Reading is the basics for all learning. (2001)
- Throughout our history, the words of the Declaration have inspired immigrants from around the world to set sail to our shores. These immigrants have helped transform thirteen small colonies into a great and growing nation of more than 300 people. (2008)
- Thank you, Your Holiness. Awesome speech. (2008)
- Families is where our nation finds hope, where wings take dream. (2002)
- If you don't stand for anything, you don't stand for anything! If you don't stand for something, you don't stand for anything! (2000)
- We ought to make the pie higher. (2000)
- Too many good docs are getting out of the business. Too many OB-GYNs aren't able to practice their love with women all across this country. (2002)
- You're working hard to put food on your family. (2000)
- There's an old saying in Tennessee—I know it's in Texas, probably in Tennessee—that says, fool me once, shame on—shame on you. Fool me—you can't get fooled again. (2002)

- I want you to know. Karyn is with us. A West Texas girl, just like me. (2004)

"Make the Pie Higher" is a poem made up solely of actual quotes from Bush. The compilation and artistic structuring of the poem is by *Washington Post* writer Richard Thompson.

MAKE THE PIE HIGHER

A poem by George W. Bush

I think we all agree, the past is over.
This is still a dangerous world.
It's a world of madmen and uncertainty
And potential mental losses.
Rarely is the question asked
Is our children learning?
Will the highways of the Internet become more few?
How many hands have I shaked?
They misunderestimate me.
I am a pitbull on the pantleg of opportunity.
I know that the human being and the fish can coexist.
Families is where our nation finds hope, where our wings
take dream.
Put food on your family!
Knock down the tollbooth!
Vulcanize society!
Make the pie higher! Make the pie higher!

Bush has been played in movies by Timothy Bottoms (twice), Kamal Haasan, James Adomian, and Josh Brolin.

CHAPTER FORTY-FOUR

BARACK OBAMA

2009– (Democrat)

Born: August 4, 1961

Presidential Term: January 20, 2009–present

Age at Inauguration: 47 years, 169 days

Vice President: Joseph R. Biden Jr.

Married: Michelle Robinson on October 18, 1992

Children: Malia Ann Obama, Natasha "Sasha" Obama

Religion: United Church of Christ

Education: Occidental College, attended 1979–1981; Columbia University, graduated 1983; Harvard Law School, graduated 1991

Occupation: Lawyer

BARACK OBAMA once said two of his favorite TV shows are *M*A*S*H* and *The Wire.*

Obama's fallback career if he couldn't make it as a politician was architect.

Obama can bench-press two hundred pounds.

Obama and former Republican vice president Dick Cheney are eighth cousins.

When Obama and his wife, Michelle, were interviewed on *60 Minutes* after winning the presidential election, Michelle was asked if Barack would wash dishes in the White House. Of course not, was the future First Lady's response. However, Obama immediately chimed in with, "I like doing dishes."

Obama's 2008 campaign slogans were "Change we can believe in," "Change," and "Hope."

Obama's nicknames include Barry, Bama, Rock, the One, and No Drama Obama.

Is Obama the first truly digital president? Presidents before Obama did not have their own computer or cell phone. Everything they did was on government equipment. Not Obama, though. He told a Univision reporter he had his own iPad and joked that as president of the United States he wasn't about to go ask someone if he could borrow their computer.

Obama's favorite movie is *Casablanca.*

Obama collects Conan the Barbarian and Spider-Man comic books.

Obama has won two Grammy Awards.

Obama and actor Brad Pitt are ninth cousins.

Obama also speaks Indonesian and Spanish.

Obama took his future wife, Michelle, to the movies on their first date. They saw Spike Lee's *Do the Right Thing.*

Obama loves playing Scrabble.

Obama is the first president born outside the forty-eight contiguous states. He was born in Honolulu, Hawaii.

Obama worked in a Baskin-Robbins as a kid and claims that because of his experiences there, to this day he cannot stand ice cream.

Obama has not been played in a movie (yet).

PRESIDENTIAL ODDS AND ENDS

What do the first fifteen presidents have in common? They were all presidents before the invention of photography so Americans had no idea what they looked like, unless they happened to see one of them in person.

There have been six presidents named James: Madison, Monroe, Polk, Buchanan, Garfield, and Carter.

Every American president has worn glasses.

The year 1881 is the only one in American history in which three presidents served. They were Rutherford B. Hayes, James Garfield, and Chester A. Arthur.

Over the years, people have reported the ghosts of Abraham Lincoln, William Henry Harrison, and Andrew Jackson haunting the White House.

According to the Secret Service, there are more threats against the First Lady than there are against the vice president.

There has never been an Italian-American president.

Mount Rushmore has the heads of George Washington, Thomas Jefferson, Abraham Lincoln, and Theodore Roosevelt and took fourteen years to sculpt. The sculptor Gutzon Borglum made the final selection of presidents to include. The original plans for the sculpture called for the four presidents to be depicted from the waist up. But time, money, and the fact that Borglum died before finishing the heads put the kibosh on that idea. His son finished the heads and they called it a day.

The Barbie doll was a presidential candidate in 1992, 2000, and 2004. (Funny, I don't remember seeing her at the debates.)

Did Shawnee chief Tecumseh curse the U.S. presidency? The Curse of Tecumseh, also known as the Zero Year Curse, states that any president elected in a year that ends in a zero would die in office. The curse seems to have been broken with the assassination attempt on Ronald Reagan, who was elected in 1980, and who survived the shooting. Presidents who seemed to satisfy the curse were William Henry Harrison (elected 1840, died 1841); Abraham Lincoln (elected 1860, died 1865); James Garfield (elected 1880, died 1881); William McKinley (elected 1900, died 1901); Warren G. Harding (elected 1920, died 1923); Franklin D. Roosevelt (elected 1940, died 1945); and John F. Kennedy (elected 1960, died 1963). As mentioned, Reagan was elected in 1980, but did not die in office. George W. Bush was elected in 2000, but did not die in office. So maybe the curse has petered out?

In the 1790s, the White House did not have any bathrooms. It did have outhouses, though.

Until the twentieth century, presidents were expected to finance all their personal needs out of the $25,000 annual salary granted them by Congress, even if they were spending their funds on government business. Several presidents left the White House broke and in a ridiculous amount of debt.

The first female candidate for U.S. president was Victoria Woodhull. She was nominated in May 1872 by the Equal Rights Party. This took guts . . . and what was probably a great sense of humor on the part of Ms. Woodhull, since women weren't even allowed to vote in 1872!

Camp David's original name was Shangri-La. President Eisenhower changed it to his grandson's name instead.

When politician Gary Hart was a candidate for president in 1988, actor Warren Beatty would routinely give him the key to his mansion and invite a number of young ladies—twenty-year-olds who were "tens"—to visit Hart, who had his pick of the bunch and indulged himself to the max. When Gary Hart's dalliance with one lady was revealed, President Reagan's response was, "Boys will be boys, but boys will not be president."

There has not been a single only-child president. Every president has had siblings.

A character on the HBO series *The Sopranos* once mistakenly referred to Benjamin Franklin as a former president.

If the president has to stay overnight in a hotel, the Secret Service prides itself on securing the president's room so that it is, literally, as safe as the White House. The president gets the entire floor of the hotel to himself. If a permanent resident of the hotel refuses to leave his or her room temporarily, then the hotel isn't used.

Vice President Dan Quayle once said, "What a waste it is to lose one's mind. Or not to have a mind is being very wasteful. How true that is."

James Polk had gas heat installed in the White House during his term. (Sure beats using wood-burning stoves for heat in a D.C. winter.) However, Polk's successor, Zachary Taylor, grew alarmed at the gas bills. They were sky-high. Could the White House really cost so much to heat? The answer, after some investigation, was no. For years, people who lived on Pennsylvania Avenue were illegally tapping into the White House's gas line. (Never let it be said that Americans aren't resourceful, right?)

John McCain's 2008 presidential campaign slogans were "Country First" and "Drill, Baby, Drill!"

THE ULTIMATE LINCOLN–KENNEDY COINCIDENCES LIST

In my 2004 book, *The Weird 100*, I compiled what I believe may be one of the most thorough and accurate lists of Lincoln–Kennedy coincidences published to date. It is a chapter that has consistently been among readers' favorites and one of the chapters for which I receive the most feedback. I am reprinting that chapter here in *Grover Cleveland's Rubber Jaw* for new readers and those interested in one of the more bizarre chapters in American presidential history.

Coincidences are spiritual puns.

—G. K. CHESTERTON

There are known to be some remarkable similarities to aspects of Presidents Lincoln's and Kennedy's lives—and deaths. Lately, more research has been done and even more commonalities in the lives and deaths of the two presidents have been uncovered.[1]

---

1. Also, one glaring error in earlier lists has been corrected. One of the coincidences that regularly made the rounds was "Lincoln's secretary was

Are all these coincidences simply due to mere chance?[2]

1. Both presidents liked rocking chairs.
2. The name of Lincoln's assassin, John Wilkes Booth, contains fifteen letters. The name of Kennedy's assassin, Lee Harvey Oswald, contains fifteen letters.
3. The name of Lincoln's successor, Andrew Johnson, contains thirteen letters. The name of Kennedy's successor, Lyndon Johnson, contains thirteen letters.
4. *Lincoln* and *Kennedy* each consist of seven letters.
5. Both presidents were named after their grandfathers.
6. Both presidents were second children.
7. Both presidents experienced the death of a sister before they became president.
8. Both presidents did not marry until they were in their thirties: Lincoln was thirty-three; Kennedy was thirty-six.
9. Both presidents married socially prominent, twenty-four-year-old brunettes who were fluent in French, known for their fashion sense, and both of whom had been previously engaged.
10. Both First Ladies oversaw major renovations of the White House.
11. Each president experienced the death of a son while president.

---

named Kennedy; Kennedy's secretary was named Lincoln." Not so. Apparently, Lincoln never had a secretary named Kennedy.

2. Special acknowledgment must go to Lu Ann Paletta and Fred L. Worth's *World Almanac of Presidential Facts*, a valuable resource in the compiling of this list.

12. The Lincoln and Kennedy children rode ponies on the White House lawn.

13. Lincoln's son Tad's funeral was held on July 16, 1871. John F. Kennedy Jr. died on July 16, 1999. Mary Todd Lincoln died on July 16, 1882. (And your author was also born on July 16 and is now writing about coincidences involving the date July 16.)

14. Two of Lincoln's sons were named Robert and Edward; two of Kennedy's brothers were named Robert and Edward.

15. Both presidents were related to U.S. senators.

16. After Lincoln was assassinated, his family moved into a house at 3014 N Street NW, in Georgetown. After Kennedy was assassinated, his family moved into a house at 3017 N Street NW, in Georgetown.

17. Both presidents were related to Democratic U.S. attorney generals who were graduates of Harvard University.

18. Both presidents were related to ambassadors to the Court of St. James in Great Britain.

19. Both presidents were friends with an Adlai E. Stevenson. Lincoln's friend would become Grover Cleveland's second vice president. Kennedy's friend would twice be the Democratic presidential nominee.

20. Both presidents knew a Dr. Charles Taft. Lincoln was treated by Dr. Charles Sabin Taft; Kennedy knew Dr. Charles Phelps Taft (the son of President Taft).

21. Both presidents were advised by a Billy Graham: Lincoln's friend was a New Salem, Illinois, schoolteacher; Kennedy's was Reverend Billy Graham.

22. Kennedy had a secretary named Evelyn Lincoln. Her husband's nickname was Abe.

23. Lincoln was first elected to the U.S. House of Representatives in 1846; Kennedy was first elected to the U.S. House of Representatives in 1946.

24. Lincoln was runner-up for his party's vice presidential nomination in 1856; Kennedy was runner-up for his party's vice presidential nomination in 1956.

25. Lincoln was elected president in 1860; Kennedy was elected president in 1960.

26. Both presidents were involved in seminal political debates: Lincoln participated in the Lincoln–Douglas debates in 1858; Kennedy participated in the Kennedy–Nixon debates in 1960.

27. Both presidents were concerned about African Americans. Lincoln wrote the Emancipation Proclamation; Kennedy submitted a report on civil rights to Congress.

28. Both presidents were writers and were well read; both presidents were versed in Shakespeare and the Bible.

29. Both had genetic diseases: Kennedy had Addison's disease; Lincoln (it is suspected) had Marfan's syndrome.

30. Both presidents were in the military.

31. Both presidents had been skippers of a boat: Lincoln had been captain of the *Talisman*; Kennedy had captained the PT-109.

32. Both presidents did not worry about their personal safety, much to the consternation of their Secret Service protection.

33. In the year of his death, Abraham Lincoln received eighty death threats in the mail. In the year of his death, John F. Kennedy received eight hundred death threats in the mail.

34. Both presidents were shot in the back of the head.

35. Both presidents were shot on a Friday before a holiday: Lincoln, Easter; Kennedy, Thanksgiving.

36. Both presidents were sitting next to their wives when they were shot.

37. Neither of the First Ladies were injured in the shootings.

38. Both presidents were with another couple when they were shot: Kennedy was with Governor and Mrs. John Connally; Lincoln was with Major and Mrs. Henry Rathbone.

39. Both of the men with the presidents, Major Rathbone and Governor Connally, were injured but not killed.

40. Lincoln was shot at Ford's Theater; Kennedy was shot in a Ford motor vehicle (a Lincoln).

41. Lincoln was shot in box seven at the theater; Kennedy was shot in car seven of his motorcade.

42. Both presidents received closed chest massage after the shooting; in both cases, it was ineffective.

43. Both presidents died in a place with the initials P.H.: Lincoln died in the Peterson House; Kennedy died in Parkland Hospital.

44. Both presidents were buried in mahogany caskets.

45. The coffins of both Lincoln and JFK were displayed in the Capitol Rotunda and the same black-draped catafalque was used for both men.

46. Both assassins were known by three names: John Wilkes Booth and Lee Harvey Oswald.

47. Both assassins were in their mid-twenties when they shot the president.

48. Both assassins had brothers with successful careers that they envied: Booth's brothers were acclaimed actors; Oswald's brothers had successful military careers.

49. Both assassins never went past the rank of private in the military.

50. Both assassins were born in the South.

51. Both assassins ideologically supported enemies of the United States: Booth supported the Confederacy; Oswald endorsed Marxism.

52. Both assassins kept a journal or diary.

53. Booth shot Lincoln in a theater (Ford's Theater) and was cornered in a warehouse; Oswald shot Kennedy from a warehouse and was cornered in a theater (the Texas Theater).

54. The concession stand operator at Ford's Theater was named Burroughs. The concession stand operator at the Texas Theater was named Burroughs.

55. Booth was aided in his escape by a man named Paine. Oswald got his job at the School Book Depository with the help of a woman named Paine.

56. Booth was trapped on Garrett's farm by an office named Baker. Oswald was questioned on the second floor of the School Book Depository by a cop named Baker.

57. Both assassins were killed by a single shot from a Colt revolver.

58. Both assassins were murdered before they could be questioned about their crimes.

59. Oswald and Booth were both shot by religious zealots: Booth by Boston Corbett; Oswald by Jack Ruby.

60. Both presidents were succeeded in office by Southern Democrats named Johnson: Lincoln, by Andrew Johnson; Kennedy by Lyndon Johnson.

61. Both Vice President Johnsons became president in their fifties: Andrew Johnson was fifty-six; Lyndon Johnson was fifty-five.

62. Andrew Johnson's father once worked as a janitor; Lyndon Johnson's father once worked as a janitor.

63. Andrew Johnson was born in 1808; Lyndon Johnson was born in 1908.

64. *Andrew* and *Lyndon* both have six letters.

65. Both President Johnsons had two daughters.

66. Both President Johnsons served in the military.

67. Both President Johnsons had previously been senators from a Southern state.

68. Both President Johnsons suffered from kidney stones.

69. The reelection opponents of both President Johnsons were men whose name began with G: Andrew Johnson against Ulysses S. Grant; Lyndon Johnson against Barry Goldwater.

70. Andrew Johnson chose not to run for reelection in 1868. Lyndon Johnson chose not to run for reelection in 1968.

THE PRESIDENTS ANAGRAM QUIZ

Here are forty-three anagrams that form the names of our presidents when unscrambled. Answers can be found on page 256.

1. SAVED FRONTIER KNOLL

   ____

2. HOMER NINJA BRAINS

   ____

3. FLORAL MIME DRILL

   ____

4. JOHN MAC ANY SQUID

   ____

5. BOA CAB KARMA

   ____

6. MAIL LOAN BRANCH

   ____

7. THEY HARBORED FURS

8. A FEDERALISM JAG

9. CORN VALVE LEDGER

10. MILKY WILL ICEMAN

11. HOVERED TOE LOOTERS

12. INDOOR OWL WOWS

13. FRESHMEN JOT SOFA

14. TRASHY RUM RAN

15. LADDER FROG

16. COGNAC DEVIL OIL

17. EGG SHOWER HUB

18. NOT SHOWING REGGAE

19. HARMONY SWIRL HAIRLINE

20. MINE JAMS SODA

21. FERN INK REPLICA

22. JOHN AM SAD

23. AN ORAL DANGER

24. REACH UTTER RASH

25. LILT INN BLOC

26. BENT RUM NIRVANA

27. MALADROIT WITH FLAW

28. SNARE ME MOJO

29. RAG HERD WARNING

30. HE OVER BROTHER

31. HUMAN JEAN SCAB

32. JENNY FED HONK

33. TRY SUNGLASSES

34. TRY JAM CRIME

35. JOCKS NEAR DAWN

____

36. PALM JOKES

____

37. TRY EL JOHN

____

38. RAIN CHORD NIX

____

39. JOHN NOW SNARED

____

40. WHITE HERO WEDDINGS

____

41. LAZY ROACH TRAY

____

42. WHOSE BUGGER

____

43. JOHN BONDS NYLON

____

ANSWERS

1. Franklin D. Roosevelt
2. Benjamin Harrison
3. Millard Fillmore
4. John Quincy Adams
5. Barack Obama
6. Abraham Lincoln

7. Rutherford B. Hayes
8. James A. Garfield
9. Grover Cleveland
10. William McKinley
11. Theodore Roosevelt
12. Woodrow Wilson
13. Thomas Jefferson
14. Harry S Truman
15. Gerald Ford
16. Calvin Coolidge
17. George H. W. Bush
18. George Washington
19. William Henry Harrison
20. James Madison
21. Franklin Pierce
22. John Adams
23. Ronald Reagan
24. Chester A. Arthur
25. Bill Clinton
26. Martin Van Buren
27. William Howard Taft
28. James Monroe
29. Warren G. Harding

30. Herbert Hoover

31. James Buchanan

32. John F. Kennedy

33. Ulysses S. Grant

34. Jimmy Carter

35. Andrew Jackson

36. James Polk

37. John Tyler

38. Richard Nixon

39. Andrew Johnson

40. Dwight D. Eisenhower

41. Zachary Taylor

42. George W. Bush

43. Lyndon B. Johnson

SOURCES AND SELECTED BIBLIOGRAPHY

Aikman, Lonnelle. *The Living White House*. Washington, D.C.: U.S. Government Printing Office, 1978.

Andrist, Ralph K. *George Washington: A Biography in His Own Words*. New York: Harper & Row, 1972.

Anthony, Carl Sferrazza. *America's First Families: An Inside View of 200 Years of Private Life in the White House*. New York: Simon & Schuster, 2000.

Benardo, Leonard, and Jennifer Weiss. *Citizen-in-Chief: The Second Lives of the American Presidents*. New York: Harper, 2009.

Beyer, Rick. *The Greatest Presidential Stories Never Told*. New York: HarperCollins, 2007.

Boller, Paul F., Jr. *Presidential Diversion: Presidents at Play from George Washington to George W. Bush*. Orlando, FL: Harcourt Books, 2007.

Caldwell, George S., ed. *Good Old Harry: The Wit and Wisdom of Harry S Truman*. New York: Hawthorn Books, 1966.

Chase, Chevy. "Mr. Ford Gets the Last Laugh." *New York Times*, January 6, 2007.

Coolidge, Calvin. *The Autobiography of Calvin Coolidge*. New York: Cosmopolitan Book Corp., 1929.

Cooper, John Milton. *Woodrow Wilson: A Biography*. New York: Alfred A. Knopf, 2009.

Crapol, Edward P. *John Tyler: The Accidental President*. Chapel Hill: University of North Carolina Press, 2006.

Current, Richard N. *The Lincoln Nobody Knows*. New York: McGraw-Hill, 1958.

Curtis, James C. *Andrew Jackson and the Search for Vindication*. Boston: Little, Brown, 1976.

DeGregorio, William A. *The Complete Book of U.S. Presidents*. Fort Lee, NJ: Barricade Books, 2009.

Ellis, Joseph J. *Passionate Sage: The Character and Legacy of John Adams*. New York: W. W. Norton, 1993.

Frank, Sid, and Arden Davis Melick. *The Presidents: Tidbits and Trivia*. New York: Greenwich House, 1977.

Frost-Knappman, Elizabeth, ed. *The World Almanac of Presidential Quotations*. New York: World Almanac, 1993.

Garrison, Webb. *Love, Lust, and Longing in the White House*. Nashville, TN: Cumberland House, 2000.

Grant, James. *John Adams: Party of One*. New York: Farrar, Strauss & Giroux, 2005.

Grantham, Dewey W., ed. *Theodore Roosevelt*. Englewood Cliffs, NJ: Prentice-Hall, 1971.

Greenberg, Davis. *Calvin Coolidge*. New York: Times Books, 2007.

Gregory, Leland H. *Presidential Indiscretions*. New York: Dell, 1999.

Hagood, Wesley O. *Presidential Sex: From the Founding Fathers to Bill Clinton*. Secaucus, NJ: Citadel Press, 1996.

Hershey, John. *The President*. New York: Alfred A. Knopf, 1975.

The History Channel. *The Presidents: The Lives and Legacies of the 43 Leaders of the United States*. New York: A&E Television Networks, 2005.

Holton, Woody. *Abigail Adams*. New York: Free Press, 2009.

Kane, Joseph Natan. *Facts about the Presidents from Washington to Johnson*. New York: H. W. Wilson, 1964.

Kennedy, Caroline, and Michael Beschloss. *Jacqueline Kennedy: Historic Conversations on Life with John F. Kennedy*. New York: Hyperion, 2011.

Kessler, Ronald. *In the President's Secret Service*. New York: Three Rivers Press, 2010.

Koch, Dora Bush. *My Father, My President: A Personal Account of the Life of George H. W. Bush*. New York: Warner Books, 2006.

Lederer, Richard. *Presidential Trivia: The Feats, Fates, Families, Foibles, and Firsts of Our American Presidents*. Layton, UT: Gibbs Smith, 2009.

Manchester, William. *One Brief Shining Moment*. Boston: Little, Brown, 1983.

McCullough, David. *Truman*. New York: Simon & Schuster, 2003.

McPherson, James M., ed. *"To the Best of My Ability": The American Presidents*. New York: Dorling Kindersley, 2000.

Melanson, Philip H. *The Secret Service: The Hidden History of an Enigmatic Agency*. New York: Carroll & Graf, 2005.

Nelson, Michael, ed. *The Presidency: A to Z*. Washington, D.C.: Congressional Quarterly, 1998.

Niven, John. *Martin Van Buren: The Romantic Age of American Politics*. New York: Oxford University Press, 1983.

Oates, Stephen B. *Abraham Lincoln: The Man behind the Myths*. New York: Harper & Row, 1984.

O'Brien, Cormac. *Secret Lives of the First Ladies*. Philadelphia: Quirk Books, 2009.

O'Brien, Cormac. *Secret Lives of the U.S. Presidents*. Philadelphia: Quirk Books, 2004.

Polk, James; Nevins, Allan, ed. *Polk: The Diary of a President, 1845–1849*. New York: Longmans, Green, 1952.

Randolph, Sarah N. *The Domestic Life of Thomas Jefferson*. Charlottesville, VA: Thomas Jefferson Memorial Foundation, 1947.

Rees, James, and Stephen Spignesi. *George Washington's Leadership Lessons*. Secaucus, NJ: John Wiley, 2007.

Reeves, Richard. *A Ford, Not a Lincoln*. New York: Harcourt Brace Jovanovich, 1975.

Sanford, Charles B. *Thomas Jefferson and His Library*. Hamden, CT: Archon Books, 1977.

Scarry, Robert J. *Millard Fillmore*. Jefferson, NC: McFarland, 2001.

Schneider, Dorothy, and Carl J. Schneider. *First Ladies: A Biographical Dictionary*. New York: Facts on File, 2005.

Shelton, Hugh General (Ret.). *Without Hesitation: The Odyssey of an American Warrior*. New York: St. Martin's Press, 2010.

Silbey, Joel H. *Martin Van Buren and the Emergence of American Popular Politics*. New York: Rowman & Littlefield, 2002.

Smith, Carter. *Presidents: Every Question Answered.* Irvington, NY: Hylas, 2004.

Smith, Jean Edward. *FDR*. New York: Random House, 2008.

Spignesi, Stephen. *The USA Book of Lists.* Secaucus, NJ: Career Press, 2000.

Spignesi, Stephen. *The Weird 100.* New York: Kensington, 2004.

Stebben, Gregg, and Jim Morris. *White House Confidential: The Little Book of Weird Presidential History.* Nashville, TN: Cumberland House, 1998.

Suburban Emergency Management Project. "Care of JFK by Dr. Max Jacobson, aka Dr. Feelgood." Biot Report #678, January 7, 2010.

Truman, Harry S. *Mr. Citizen*. New York: Popular Library, 1961.

Truman, Harry S. *Truman Speaks: On the Presidency, the Constitution, and Statecraft*. New York: Columbia University Press, 1975.

Truman, Margaret. *Letters from Father.* New York: Arbor House, 1981.

ACKNOWLEDGMENTS

First, I'd like to thank my literary agent John White, who always loved this book and worked diligently to find the right home for it. I'd also like to express boundless thanks and love to my sweetie, Valerie, and I'd also like to thank my biggest fan, my mother, Lee Spignesi Mandato. My editor, Jeanette Shaw, deserves special praise for everything she did to see this book shepherded into print. I've done several books for Penguin over the years and every one has been a joy to work on. Jeanette continues the Penguin tradition of being a terrific, supportive editor and a professional who helped make this book better than I could have done alone. My thanks also to everyone on the *Grover Cleveland's Rubber Jaw* team, particularly for your help, advice, and meticulous attention to making the book as good as it could be.

My cherished friends George Beahm, Kevin Quigley, Jim Cole, Kathy Marotto, and Rachel Montgomery all deserve singling out for special thanks.

I'd also like to thank the University of New Haven, a place where I am honored to teach, and to mention especially the wonderful staff of the Marvin K. Peterson Library, in particular, Diane Spinato and Joseph Fox.

I'd also like to thank the Library of Congress for their stalwart efforts in ensuring that photos of our history are available to all and preserved for the ages.

I also thank my dear brother from another mother and writing partner, Mike Lewis; my beloved friend and writing partner, the charming and always effervescent Adrienne Candela; Dr. Donald M. Smith at UNH and Dr. Russell Gaudio at Gateway; my dearly loved Uncle Steve and Aunt Marge; and all my students, past and present, who expressed an interest in this book and promised to buy it. (Ahem.)

ABOUT THE AUTHOR

STEPHEN SPIGNESI is a *New York Times* bestselling author who writes about historical biography, popular culture, television, film, American and world history, and contemporary fiction. He is also a university professor, novelist, poet, screenwriter, and musician.

Spignesi—dubbed "the world's leading authority on Stephen King" by *Entertainment Weekly* magazine—has worked with Stephen King, Turner Entertainment, the Margaret Mitchell estate, Andy Griffith, the Smithsonian Institution, George Washington's Mount Vernon, Viacom, and other personalities and entities on a broad range of projects. Spignesi has also contributed essays, chapters, articles, and introductions to a wide range of books.

Spignesi's more than fifty books have been translated into several languages, including Chinese, Polish, French, Italian, Farsi, and Indonesian, and he has also written for *Harper's, Cinefantastique, Saturday Review, TV Guide, Mystery Scene, Gauntlet,* and *Midnight Graffiti* magazines as well as the *New York Times,* the *New York Daily News,* the *New York Post,* the *New Haven Register,* the

French literary journal *Tenébres,* and the Italian online literary journal *Horror.It.*

Spignesi has also appeared on CNN, MSNBC, Fox News Channel, and other TV and radio outlets; in the 1998 E! documentary *The Kennedys: Power, Seduction, and Hollywood* as a Kennedy family authority; and in the A&E *Biography* of Stephen King that aired in January 2000. Spignesi's 1997 book *J.F.K. Jr.* was a *New York Times* bestseller. Spignesi's *Complete Stephen King Encyclopedia* was a 1991 Bram Stoker Award nominee.

In addition to writing, Spignesi also lectures on a variety of popular culture and historical subjects and is a Practitioner in Residence at the University of New Haven in Connecticut where he teaches English composition and literature, writing, and courses on Stephen King and the *Titanic.* He is also an Adjunct Professor of English at Gateway Community College in Connecticut. He is the founder and editor in chief of the small press publishing company The Stephen John Press. Spignesi was recently praised for "reinventing the psychological thriller" upon the publication of his acclaimed debut novel, *Dialogues.*

His website is www.stephenspignesi.com.

His Facebook page is www.facebook.com/stephen.spignesi.

Spignesi lives in New Haven, Connecticut, with his gray cat, Chloe.